Beyond
"Thank You
for Your Service"

The Veteran Champion handbook for civilians

Lt. Col. Kathy Lowrey Gallowitz
U.S.A.F. Retired

Kathy@VanguardVeteran.com
Ordering Information:
Quantity sales. Special discounts are available on quantity purchases by corporations, associations, and others. For details, contact the publisher at the address above.

 www.VanguardVeteran.com

Paperback:ISBN: 978-0-578-67709-5

Printed in the United States of America.

CONTENTS

1. What is a Veteran Champion? 5

2. Cultivating Veteran Champions 14

3. The Impact of Military Culture 27

4. Employers 45

5. The Faith Community.....................................78

6. The Legal Community 94

7. The Healthcare Community6...........................103

8. Community Influencers 122

9. The Education Community 134

10. Resources 146

Beyond
"Thank You
for Your Service"

The Veteran Champion handbook for civilians

Lt. Col. Kathy Lowrey Gallowitz

U.S.A.F. Retired

1. What is a Veteran Champion?

> *The willingness with which our young people are likely to serve in any war no matter how justified shall be directly proportional to how they perceive the Veterans of earlier wars, were treated and appreciated by their nation.~ attributed to George Washington*

My heart's desire is to inspire you to reach out and assist with the needs of our Veterans. Through stories shared in the following pages, you'll see where it's a simple matter to step into this role—but life affirming and life-changing to the Veteran and Military Connected Person.

For the purposes of this book, when we say **Servicemembers or Veterans,** we include those who are serving or have served in a military branch of the U.S. Armed Forces: members currently serving on active duty and in the reserve component, those separated or retired from the active force, Reserve, Guard, and Individual Mobilization Augmentees, from combat to medical and *everything* in between. **Military Connected Persons** (MCP) includes those who love someone who wears or wore a military uniform: a spouse, their children, parents, siblings, extended family such as cousins, aunts, uncles, and grandparents.

A Veteran Champion is a civilian advocate primarily for the Servicemember or Veteran but includes Military Connected Persons. A Veteran Champion appreciates the sacrifice and service of our Military and reaches out to Servicemembers as an employer, friend, neighbor, a support and/or liaison. They're grateful to assist in making the transition from military to civilian life smoother, less lonely and to welcome them "all the way home." Veteran Champions have not served and may or may not be related to those who have.

A Veteran Champion is a civilian with a basic understanding of military culture who speaks effectively into the life of a Veteran or MCP and has meaningful, mutually beneficial interactions. They understand the unique dynamic of military life and anticipate how to assist them.

The Veteran Champion comes alongside MCP when someone in their household deploys.

They're not afraid to ask questions or be available. And they're part of the welcoming committee when the Servicemember returns or separates from duty.

A Veteran Champion intentionally chooses Veterans and MCP to invest in by extending friendship, sharing time, resources, and personal networks.

Veteran Champions educate themselves about military culture and how to leverage knowledge and resources more effectively. They help bridge gaps between military and civilian life: at work as a co-worker or employer, as an educator, healthcare provider, attorney, or in another capacity. A Veteran Champion supports Veterans by showing, through action, how much their service and sacrifice is appreciated.

This book shares big and small ways Veteran Champions have impacted the military community. A Veteran Champion isn't all things to all people. They do what they're able for neighbors and people in their sphere of influence. Many of these ideas can be springboards into creating greater ways to champion our Military personnel. My best advice is to lead with your heart.

Why is this Important?

Because our Vietnam Veterans suffered, and continue to suffer, we learned some very hard lessons. They were drafted for Vietnam; forced to fight a war that a high percentage of Americans didn't agree with. When they came back—if they came back—they were mistreated and then forgotten. Not surprisingly, they felt abandoned by America.

With Vietnam in the rearview mirror, our government strategically mobilized the Guard and Reserve component in response to the First Gulf War and 9/11. Now our Armed Forces are volunteers. They represent our neighbors, bankers, bakers, and candlestick makers. They're people we know personally and have had relationship with before going to war. When those Reserve and Guard volunteers are absent, we see evidence of being at war; there's a visible and felt impact in our local communities. Civilians feel more invested, a sense of ownership, an increased awareness that "one of ours" is over there and we want them home. When they do come home, we're less likely to ignore them. With this change, it's important to become aware of Veterans' needs and get involved.

Transitions out of Military service present different levels of difficulty. The loss of personal networks, loss of purpose and meaning, and the loss of identity is felt almost immediately. The transition from this life to the next can be made more smoothly and peacefully with the help of Veteran Champions.

On a large scale, this country loves its Veterans and appreciates their sacrifices. Most civilians want to support Servicemembers which is evidenced by nearly 40,000 non-profit Veteran support organizations across the nation. Events like one day marksmanship camps, horse-riding, and car-racing, help raise awareness and promote connectivity. Meaningful relationships are often developed, but we need more: a robust, consistent network of prepared civilian neighbors and experts who are ready and willing to support Veterans and their families.

When civilians are more informed, know what the needs are and how they can assist, they're more than willing to contribute; they show up and show out in amazing ways. We'll showcase civilians who looked at their circle of influence and leveraged those connections to support our Veterans.

While doing outreach for the Guard throughout the state of Ohio, I learned about a lot of great programs. Despite all that is being done, it's simply impossible for the Veterans Administration (VA) and Department of Defense (DOD) to meet all the needs of every Veteran without the help of the citizenry. Government programs are being overhauled to assist currently transitioning Veterans, but they're in their infancy and often cumbersome. Local communities can be nimbler and more responsive.

We learned really tough lessons from Vietnam. To avoid repeating those mistakes, each one of us must show our gratitude to those sacrificing so much—for us.

What's at Stake?

We don't have to look very far to see how fragmented our country has become and the ripple effects of isolation: addiction, loneliness, mistrust and escalating suicide rates. And the COVID-19 pandemic only made it worse. By not championing our Veterans we promote not only their isolation, but our own. We alienate the very people we depend on to defend us. If you're reading this book, you already want to make changes. If we don't actively build bridges with each other, our country is in trouble.

Our love for and trust in Military personnel gives us a solid place from which to build new relationships. Who better to connect with and begin repairing the social fabric of society than our military members who defend and protect our freedom? Who better to create a friendship with than someone who exemplifies honor, loyalty, and duty?

In the following chapters, you'll read accounts of various people who felt compelled to do something for Servicemembers. Their acts of kindness toward the Veteran and Military Connected community changed lives on both sides forever, in positive, mutually beneficial ways. In reading these accounts, you'll see examples of ways you will enrich your life as you enrich the lives of Veterans and their families.

Why Now?

Nearly 2.6 million Iraq and Afghanistan Veterans have fought since 9/11. When they return from military service, many carry visible and invisible wounds. Their families, who also make sacrifices, are affected by their absence and then again by their return. Many of these warriors and their families who have been paying the price for our freedom, have unmet needs. And, many Veterans from previous conflicts continue to struggle.

At one end of the continuum, our Veterans need to be better prepared to find and keep a meaningful, mission-focused career after military service. In years past, Servicemembers only received four to five days of job search preparation training. This will be further explained in Chapter 4. At the other end, some have no family support and carry physical and emotional injuries; 11-20% of Iraq and Afghanistan Veterans—and nearly 30% from Vietnam—have Post Traumatic Stress Disorder (PTSD.) It is important to emphasize here that most Veterans are highly resilient; more than 80% of Iraq and Afghanistan and 70% of Vietnam Veterans DO NOT have PTSD.

Every year, nearly 200,000 persons separate from military service. Virtually half feel disconnected from mainstream America. Veteran Champions help bridge those gaps.

Our national defense is everyone's business. Our country will always need defenders. When one considers that only three out of ten U.S. citizens are fit and eligible for military service, every citizen who does not serve has a moral obligation to aid and assist those who do. We're all in this together.

2. Cultivating Veteran Champions

It hit me, at the age of forty, while attending the funeral of a businessman who'd been killed on a jet ski, that I'd never had this experience. Besides family, I hadn't been to a funeral. I began reflecting on the differences between military and civilian life. My entire existence had been centered on growing up in a military family and serving in the military.

The military community is generally young and healthy. Because I hadn't been to combat, I hadn't seen much death. I had moved a lot and not been in a community long enough to know people who died. Which means, it's unlikely that I'd know the lady down the street, who had been battling cancer for several years. If I felt this kind of disconnection from mainstream America, I wondered if other military members were also experiencing this?

When I was new in town, I was focused on necessities: How to get to work? Find a hairdresser. Where to get groceries? Where to get the car fixed? Anyone who moves a lot can relate.

This led to another observation: I didn't understand how America worked. I didn't know what a city council was or what a county commissioner did. I'd taken civics and government courses—but if you're highly mobile, you probably aren't going to be around for the next local election. Or, if you happen to be, you may not be knowledgeable about or connected to the people or issues enough to know how to cast your vote.

For military people and their families, the military is their community. Moving a lot is a big part of that life. Life is filtered through a different grid: military training, mindset, language, and experience. We typically live and breathe "all things military," especially if you grew up in and served in the active duty component. Our perspectives are usually different and the way we relate to each other is often different than the way civilians interact with each other.

These differences become obvious when Veterans separate from active service and step into civilian life. By then, their network is scattered across the nation, if not across the world. When they seek employment or need legal assistance, if they want to be part of a faith community or want coffee with a friend, they realize they need something the military isn't equipped to give them—a civilian network.

At that funeral, I felt disconnected. I knew I was American but felt like I didn't belong because my experiences were different. How odd that those of us who are passionate about serving our country, who sacrifice for it, are the same ones who feel like they don't fit in when they quit relocating or return from war. That's not right! It's particularly acute when there's a crisis and no one in your local community notices. And there's no one who's close by to reach out to for help.

We all need a hand occasionally, someone to lean on when we hurt. It's a struggle moving into a new neighborhood and needing or wanting a friend and having no one to turn to. The well-ingrained values and ethos of military culture also complicate trying to decide whether to untangle from a toxic relationship.

Additionally, the loss of military identity affects our sense of purpose. If a Veteran can't find the right-fit career, their quality of life is affected. That mismatch disappoints him or her and the employer.

A Veteran who feels disconnected, may become isolated and depressed. Veterans struggling post-service with physical or mental ailments that go undetected and untreated, can end up in the legal system, homeless or worse— suicidal.

You may wonder, why don't they get help? Do they know what services and benefits are available to them? How to access it? Civilians who know how to connect Veterans with the benefits they've earned and services they need could make an enormous impact in that life.

A Veteran (like anyone else) needs a network, a lifeline, a friend, in place when they're in trouble. Through the Veteran Champion movement, I envision civilians anticipating and supporting Veterans, thereby preventing trouble. A Veteran Champion can be the difference between a life cut short or one well-lived.

This burgeoning awareness triggered something within me. If I felt disconnected even though I'm outgoing, articulate, and assertive how lonely and difficult might it be for Servicemembers without those abilities? I knew how to build connections with strangers anywhere and create a satisfying life—I'd been doing it since I was born. It's a matter of survival for a military child.

It occurred to me that I could help civilians learn to build bridges with Veterans. Hardly anyone does this important work! The opportunity to bridge this gap invigorated me. I enjoy articulating new ideas, identifying practical solutions, bringing people together, and encouraging them to make a difference. Informing and engaging civilians in support of Servicemembers and Veterans is my life's calling, and why I developed

Vanguard Veteran to equip civilians to become Veteran Champions.

Civilians Care and Want to Help

I've seen how eager civilians are to assist—but often they don't know where to begin. Those who haven't served don't understand how mindset and value differences create culture gaps. The difference between military and civilian life can affect a Veterans' ability to reintegrate into America. No training exists to help them return to civilian life. It's exacerbated when Military Connected Persons live on a military base in a foreign country. I have experienced this firsthand.

I am third generation military. I was born into an active duty Navy family, in Pensacola, Florida while dad was a pilot in training. Soon afterward, we were assigned to Paris, France, where we lived in a five-story, brick, mansion with a wine cellar. My bedroom had fifteen-foot tall ceilings, a fireplace, and a wrought-iron balcony overlooking acres of countryside. As a five-year-old, I thought the house was spooky.

While attending a French-speaking preschool, I learned the language fluently. Already, my entire DNA was being influenced by my father's military career. One of my earliest childhood memories is as a seven-year-old in 1966, sailing into New York Harbor on the USS United States. Holding my mother's hand, I waved to the Statue of Liberty. Looking up at the gorgeous statue, I didn't understand what she represented, but she made a big impression. Then, I went to an English-speaking kindergarten. My dad said I struggled to learn my native tongue. After that, we moved every three or four years.

As an adult, I've worked seventeen different civilian and military jobs in six different industries. Before the age of thirty-five, I'd lived in at least twenty different communities. Through many moves, I learned how meaningful it is to have a network of support. Having strong connectivity and a sense of belonging brings me great joy and immense gratitude. Up until the time I moved to Ohio in 1993, I had experienced community and network support in short bursts. Everywhere I went, I had to reinvent myself and my life, make new connections, new friends, and find new jobs. Military people and others who move a lot are great at starting over. They're great at first impressions. Every new place is another chance to make it all work, meet new people and create a new life.

Because of my mobile way of life, I felt that I was "skimming the surface" of life. But these experiences taught me unique insights that later helped Veteran Champions better serve those who serve our country.

My First Veteran Champion

At Lackland Air Force Base in San Antonio, Texas, I met my first husband at a patient's bedside in Wilford Hall Medical Center's Intensive Care Unit where I worked. We were both on active duty in the United States Air Force, me a nurse, he a physician. Early in our marriage, balancing a dual military career with the rotating shifts required in healthcare proved challenging. I had dreamed of becoming Chief of the Nurse Corp. But before long, we agreed (me with a heavy heart) that I would leave active military service in the best interests of our family and anticipated children.

Our marriage had been difficult from the onset. Though disappointed I thought I can "do" difficult. I made a commitment! I naively believed that I could make this work. I was more than willing to do whatever it took because I loved my husband and wanted our marriage to succeed.

Over our eighteen-year marriage, we withstood the rigors of surgical residency, another year of subspecialty training, creating a medical practice (from scratch!) having three sons in five years, in addition to my obligations to the Air Force Reserve and moving six times. This was demanding enough but they weren't the toughest of times.

Then our middle son was diagnosed with Acute Lymphocytic Leukemia at the age of two. Subsequently, he received four years of treatment. (Twenty-six years later he's the "poster child" for childhood cancer survival.) Following that, was my husband's diagnosis—which finally gave me insight into why I found our marriage so stressful. *But, what could I do about it*?

I struggled for most of the marriage trying to decide whether to leave. There were always more pressing priorities. Much of the time was spent trying to resolve the next crisis or addressing the next demand of the day. And fundamentally, both my Christian and military values heavily influenced my judgment. I didn't want to violate covenants I'd made to God or commitments I'd made to my husband and children. I took this and the military value of "Service before self!" very seriously. I was determined to make it work. And why not? I had been able to do it in other areas of my life: growing up with alcoholic parents, a strict father and moving every three or four years. Those lessons taught me that "I can deal, I'll be okay, I'll figure it out and that I'll make it work." This thinking had been groomed by military upbringing, military culture. As a result, I had an unrealistic view of what I could handle and how and when to be loyal.

My mother died just before I delivered my first child. My father lived out of state and—due to constantly moving—I didn't have many friends or a support network to help me navigate marriage difficulties. And, I was very stoic, almost stubbornly so.

An astute Veteran Champion is critical when the Servicemember has little family support and no civilian network. Remember that Servicemembers are doggedly independent and don't ask for help easily—even at their own expense.

A couple of times at my wit's end, I went to counseling just to confirm that I really wasn't crazy... but that relief was short-lived. At the end of the day, I felt abused and violated. I began believing I couldn't make the marriage work. Sadly, and it took a long time and a tragic event for me to leave.

Because of the unexpected support of a Veteran Champion from my church, I recovered. I'm immensely grateful for Laura and her impact on my life. She helped me fully appreciate the power of a caring neighbor and how Veteran Champions truly can be lifesavers.

During the divorce, Laura showed up—a kind-hearted, civilian woman who made a life-changing difference in my quality of life. She showed up in the darkest of times when I needed a friend the most. Besides my sister Kim, she was my first Veteran Champion—although I didn't call her that at the time.

Other Pieces Come Together

My second husband's perspective and experience is different than mine. His transition from active duty military changed his identity overnight. He spent twenty-five years proudly serving the U.S. Army, and traveling around the world. As a commander for most of his career, when he walked into the room, people stood up to show respect. Then, Ed stepped into civilian life where very few people knew him, and no one stood up.

As an active duty Soldier and combat Veteran, his network was his battle buddies. No one can replace a battle buddy. When we married—although his four grown children live in Tennessee—he moved to Columbus to start our new life together and re-invent himself.

I never went to combat. As a female officer, I served alongside 85% men, mostly physicians and pilots. Military culture frowns upon officers fraternizing with male or female enlisted personnel and expects everyone to maintain a professional distance with superiors. Meaning that during twenty-years of full-time military service, I usually ate lunch alone. All the moving and many different jobs resulted in few long-term relationships.

The strength of my military network is nothing like the strength of Ed's though they both provide connection and a strong sense of belonging. This military network helps little with building your civilian one. Now, Ed is building his from scratch. Every day he feels the loss of a much-loved career with meaning and purpose.

Active duty and Reserve duty retirements and transitions are different, as are transitions for combat and non-combat Veterans. The experiences and perspectives of Ed and his battle buddies gave me insight into how Veterans struggle "coming home" and how they succeed. Their approaches exemplify highly resilient, and ideal ways to overcome transition struggles and build satisfying lives.

People Who Want to Help are Everywhere

The needs of Military Connected Persons can be great and far reaching. For instance, the military spouses whose mobility and sparse job history makes finding and keeping employment difficult; those who have lost family members to war or military training accidents; or the vast number of caregivers attending to our nation's injured warriors.

With government agencies unable to keep up, we need every American citizen to connect with and purposefully support their Veterans and Military Connected Persons. We need YOU to become a Veteran Champion.

It's easier than you think!

At a recent neighborhood gathering, I met a woman whose father was a celebrated World War II Veteran and a Purple Heart recipient.

"How can I help Veterans?" she asked.

"It's really quite simple," I replied. "Find out who the Servicemembers are at your job, place of worship and in your neighborhood. Take interest in them. Get to know them. Ask open-ended questions about their time in the military and let them take the conversation where they want. Then, ask what you can do to support them and do it!"

"That's a great idea!" she said. "I can do that!"

I bet she will!

3. The Impact of Military Culture

"Oh no, dad, are you kidding me? We have to move again? Move overseas? I've been here for seven years. I don't want to go. I'm so comfortable here. I feel like I belong." I remember where I was sitting and what we were all doing in that moment, because I wasn't ready to up and move. In a blink, my whole world felt like it was shifting sideways.

"I know this is going to be really hard on you," my dad said. "I did everything I could to stay here, at The Pentagon. But the Navy's sending me where they need me. It's a great opportunity for my career. I'll be the Commanding Officer of a Naval communications station on an island in the north Atlantic Ocean, monitoring Russian submarine traffic. You know how this works, honey. We've been in the Navy a long time. It's about the needs of the Navy."

My dad could probably tell what I was thinking: as wonderful as that was for him, it didn't feel so wonderful for me. Although I hadn't had to think about it for a long time, I was quickly dusting off my unwritten list of things this move would cost me. I wasn't a little kid with a suitcase of "missing my friends" memories. I was older now, and I had developed a whole life apart from my parents and the military. Before I could gather my thoughts, he shifted gears.

"This will be a great mind-broadening experience for you. Most people don't live like they do here in Fairfax, Virginia. You'll have an opportunity to learn a lot about the world."

"But, Dad—"

"And oh, by the way, you'll probably be a big fish in a small pond because you'll go to a small Department of Defense high school on a military base."

What? Was that supposed to be good news? Now it was my turn to speak.

"Dad," I said, "My pond here is just fine. Let me tell you about my life. I am so happy here. You know why? I've got friends, I love hanging out under the streetlight in front of our house— we hang out a couple of times a week. I don't have to worry who I'm having lunch with in the school cafeteria because I have scads of friends. That is an incredible feeling. I love my swim team—my butterfly stroke is even getting better. The coach gave me the Coaches Award for my sportsmanship. I'm about to finish my Girl Scout Gold award. That's a prestigious award! I've *got* to finish that before we leave." I couldn't tell if this was changing his mind, or if he understood how important all this was, but he didn't stop me, so I kept going.

"We've been here for so long, that I even have some traditions with Nancy, next-door. Every year, we share each other's Christmas presents, and swap baked goods—I love these traditions. And, I just turned sixteen. I can finally drive on my own. I was really looking forward to this added independence. Living on a small island in the north Atlantic Ocean, where they speak a foreign language, where am I going to be able to drive there? Nowhere! That's the pits!

"If losing all that isn't hard enough, being a cheerleader has become my identity. I love it. There's already been rumblings next year, as a senior, I could be captain of the varsity cheer-leading squad in a class of four hundred! And there's a good chance that will come true. Are they going to have cheerleading on some base in the North Atlantic? Probably not." I slumped back in my chair. It's true, I was really feeling sorry for myself. We had moved before, but now that I was older, moving cost me much more.

My dad had patiently listened to all I had to say without even flinching. We'd been in this place before, feeling sad, not wanting to leave, but this time it was different. Fairfax had been our home for seven years and I loved it. My feelings didn't really figure too much into the equation. Every time dad got new orders, the result was always the same. I notified friends, we cried, my family and I prepared for moving day, then we shipped out to the next place. And started all over again.

"Alright," dad said. He had another idea up his sleeve, and he didn't seem quick to share it. "Maybe you can stay here and live with another family and graduate with your classmates. Would you like to do that?"

I must have looked incredulous. I had been so busy resisting, reliving other moves, that I hadn't been looking at other options. I didn't know I had options! In that moment, I didn't know what I wanted to do.

"Think about it," he said.

I left that conversation a little more empowered, at least, enough to consider it for a couple months. After weighing my options, I went back to my parents.

"You know, I'm leaving home in a year and a half and going off to college. Plus, mom and I are really close; I feel like she needs me. So, I'm going with you guys."

It still makes me a little emotional, but I remember it like it was yesterday. Fifteen or twenty of my friends came to say goodbye at the airport. As the plane pulled away from the gate at Dulles, I sobbed. I left Fairfax, flew over the ocean, and landed at a military base in Keflavik, Iceland. Yikes, welcome to my new world. Everything had just turned upside-down.

But Dad was right. I became a "big fish," even though it didn't feel like it, nor did I care about such things, that's just who I was. At Alfred T. Mahan High School, I started a cheerleading squad and became the captain. By then, cheerleading—encouraging, precision, teamwork—were big parts of my personality. My senior class of thirty people elected me president. Because I'd moved so much, I knew how to leverage first impressions and make the best of things.

After graduation, I attended the University of Maryland in Munich, Germany then Mary Washington College in Fredericksburg, Virginia completing two years of nursing school prerequisites. I then went to the two-year baccalaureate nursing degree program at the Medical College of Virginia in Richmond.

On day one of nursing school we were all strangers. I'd stick out my hand and say, "Hi, I'm Kathy." I later followed with "I'd like to be your class president." And you know what? I was president both years. At my commencement ceremony, I was the honored recipient of the Dean Doris B. Yingling Leadership Award.

My desire to lead began at twelve in Girl Scouts, when someone saw my potential. I've aspired to leadership roles ever since.

What it Means

Military culture equals the sum of all knowledge, beliefs, morals, customs, habits, and capabilities acquired by Servicemembers and their families through membership in military organizations. Everything about my life has been influenced by the military. Service and the military mindset is encoded in my DNA.

Military life requires vastly different skill sets and mindsets than civilian life. Military training conditions new Servicemembers to integrate seamlessly into military life. We're immersed in the values and culture necessary to help us function in war. Uncle Sam spends a lot of time and money training military members in highly structured environments how to do their job, function as teams, and lead. Characteristics of military service can be slightly different between branches.

We're trained to never leave a fallen comrade behind, and this instills in each of us a moral code. We internalize mission above self. "We" not "me," is the selflessness we willingly adopt. We rely on teammates and self to "get 'er done." We are loyal to a fault. We're driven to pursue excellence. We learn to be patient and never quit.

Stoicism becomes deeply ingrained, and more so in those with combat experience and longer military service. Out of necessity, military training changes thinking and behavior.

The U.S. Armed Forces

Army: Soldiers serve in this oldest and largest force that stabilizes land.

Navy: Sailors deter aggression and maintain freedom of the seas.

Coast Guard: Coast Guardsmen serve in this oldest continuous seagoing service that defends and protects ports and harbors, provides search and rescue and is part of the Navy during wartime.

Marines: Marines are part of the Navy and serve as America's expeditionary force fighting swiftly and aggressively on land, air, and sea.

Air Force: Airmen strive to maintain air superiority and expand the capabilities of other forces.

Space Force: This newest branch of the armed forces was established December 20, 2019. It is an independent service focused on protecting U.S. and allied interests in space and providing space capabilities to the joint force.

Types of Duty within Service Branches

- **Active Duty Members**: Full-time
  About 1.3 million

- **Selected Reserve Members**
  National Guard and Reserve: About 802,800
  - **Guard:** Army and Air Force; called to active duty deployments and state emergencies
  - **Reserve:** Army, Navy, Marine Corps, Air Force, Coast Guard; called to active duty deployments
  - **Both:** Monthly drills and yearly 2-week Annual Training; Pre 9/11 were part-time

- **Veterans:** Separated or Retired
  Nearly 17% retire after serving twenty years
  Overall 19,000,000
  - Approximately 7,000,000 from Vietnam era
  - About 2,600,000 from Iraq/Afghanistan era

Military cultural differences become clear when compared to civilian culture.

Cultural Differences

Military:
- Strict hierarchy
- Emphasis on teamwork

- Orderly and focused
- Tough and physical
- Controlled/unemotional
- Highly disciplined
- Value aggression
- Values: Integrity and honor
- Reliance on authority
- Feeling unsafe

Civilian:
- All are equal
- Emphasis more on self
- Easy going
- Comfortable
- Emotions expressed
- Relatively undisciplined
- Aggression not valued
- Values: Getting ahead
- Skeptical of authority
- Feeling safe

Military culture affects Servicemembers for the rest of our lives. It can manifest in a reluctance to ask for or seek help, delaying the pursuit of medical care, minimizing, or denying a circumstance that is painful or difficult. Many believe needing or getting help implies weakness. (I'm optimistic that this is changing.) Because we're conditioned to "tough it out," this can be detrimental post-service.

The impact of these principles plays out more acutely in the warrior, a Servicemember who's been in combat. Stoicism is a golden asset if you're at war. Because of selflessness, they're usually more concerned about the welfare of others at the expense of their own safety. In a warrior's desire to pursue excellence, anything short of it can leave them feeling ashamed. Losing a comrade often results in grief, complicated by survivor's guilt. Warriors may falsely believe they could have positively affected circumstances which were, in fact, beyond their control. Potentially, shame occurs in response to these unrecognized or misunderstood feelings of helplessness. In civilian life, it may translate into suffering silently, ignoring symptoms that arise from deep wounding.

Transitioning out of the Military

One major question Servicemembers face after separating from military is, "Who am I now?" They must acknowledge and grieve many losses. They leave a place of comradeship and purpose for civilian culture where they feel alienated and unsure where they fit in. They trade a highly structured environment and predictable routine, for an unstructured environment where everything must be figured out. Reluctance to ask for help makes this highly stressful time during transition more difficult.

Second Nature

Through military training we acquire a high level of job training, strong core values, and adaptability. We willingly trust and have faith in co-workers and are usually trustworthy and honest to a fault. We respect authority. We're committed to our organizations, are loyal to our family, friends, and peers. For Veterans, teamwork is a way of life.

We embrace a "can-do" attitude, we're flexible and excited to learn new things. We aren't strangers to change. We've traveled a lot, worked with people from around the world and are routinely inclusive. We pride ourselves on community involvement.

We learn to be highly disciplined, orderly, and mission focused. Veterans echo these attributes in their organizations, actions, and communications. We take all we've learned and leverage it to benefit our team. It's practically automatic.

Veterans make excellent entrepreneurs and employers. My first husband and I started a medical practice. Because of military training, we're avid learners willing to try new things. Taking informed risks is part of our nature. Our confidence is reflected in our resilience, agility, and quick-thinking under pressure. We're undaunted by challenges. We want to create processes and procedures and see a mission through to the end. Most importantly, we want everyone on our team to succeed.

When my first husband was ready to leave active duty, he was working at Kirtland Air Force Base in Albuquerque, New Mexico. Truthfully, we could have lived almost anywhere we wanted because surgeons are in demand everywhere. Having lived so many places, I knew life is what you make it, and wherever you are, you meet great people and can make a new life.

My husband attended the Ohio State University College of Medicine. He didn't like Ohio winters, and didn't want to live there. Out of nowhere, I received a phone call from an independent surgeon at Fairfield Medical Center in Lancaster, Ohio.

When I hung up, I said, "Let's go check this out."

We had already decided to live somewhere else. We'd signed a contract, taken a sign-on bonus and purchased a big house. But when we visited Lancaster, I just fell in love with it. The Square 13 Historic District with the gazebo and beautiful homes was charming. Fairfield Medical Center was a good hospital and the school system good for our kids. We were in a small town near a big city. During previous visits to my in-laws, I'd formed a good impression of the Midwest because of their family values and work ethic. I loved the idea of living in small-town America, re-creating that longed-for sense of belonging, and living the "American Dream." Then I learned about Lancaster's music festival. Wow, these people really care about their community, I thought. They're civic-minded; I want to live in a community like that.

I wanted to achieve two objectives: Give our children roots, (because I never had them) and start a business and have a military career. Lancaster impressed me as a place where we could do both beautifully and live a long time. I'm grateful to this day that my spouse was willing to change plans.

I participated in every aspect of the medical practice (except for surgery) learning as I went. Having dealt with so much change and different experiences as a military member, I had the confidence and willingness to take on this new challenge.

Neither of us had been to business school, nor did we know anything about civilian healthcare reimbursement. We hired people with that expertise. I insisted on having the reception, business office and patient care staffs in different uniforms. We created, taught, and enforced business policies and procedures and closely monitored receivables. We learned office management best practices from Mount Carmel's medical professional services. Key staff leaders and I attended dozens of courses. We educated ourselves and applied what we learned, and our discipline paid off. Without the drive, discipline, and self-confidence learned in the military, I doubt I would've embraced the challenge.

We used two models: In the military we train, we apply. In medicine: "see one, do one, teach one." You learn how to do something, go do it, then you train somebody else to do it. And it worked!

In six years, the business grew from one doctor and three staff in one county to three doctors and twenty-five staff in three counties. We hired Veterans for two key positions: The Physician Assistant and Clinic Manager. My husband was a workaholic, and those two kept right up with him. The rest of this team, particularly the Billing Manager and Office Manager, worked hard, too.

Our small business strengthened the community and local economy. We served countless patients, as volunteer leaders in local chambers of commerce, created jobs and donated financially to local organizations. The Lancaster Fairfield Chamber of Commerce awarded me the Small Businessperson of the Year.

It Runs Deep

Recognizing the skillsets and behaviors needed to run a business is one thing, it's quite another to understand how military culture impacts your personality and thinking. I didn't understand how much I had been influenced, until I took (and then taught) the Center for Deployment Psychology's behavioral health provider military culture course.

Without a support network, my Christian values and military experience led to unrealistic thinking, when my personal beliefs were violated, and my safety threatened. I struggled for years in my marriage trying to discern whether my commitment, loyalty, sense of duty, and service-before-self were misplaced.

Why had I stayed in a difficult relationship? Was it because I didn't know how to be vulnerable with other women who could help me? It was not. I cultivated friendships quickly.

When it came to forming personal relationships, the trick was investing that perfect amount of myself so that it didn't hurt as much when it came time to move again. For sure, it was a delicate balancing act. And it never worked.

It came down to a few basic questions: Who knew me well enough to help? Who had known us long enough to say, "Hey, whoa! This isn't quite right." When you're transient, people don't get enough time to really know you. They don't see the development of problems. They take you at face value.

One day, while struggling through the aftermath of leaving my first marriage, Laura seemingly just appeared. We'd met through church. We had no history together. She knew I needed help and went out of her way to offer it. She became my rock. To this day, she is my best friend.

Laura was my Veteran Champion because she found me and supported me. She knew nothing about military service or military culture. She's a good Christian woman and an exceptional person. She's one of those rare people who a) can do anything, b) demonstrates her faith in God through service to others, c) knows instinctively when and how to serve people and d) willingly goes out of her way to do it.

As a single mother herself, she watched my children in my home, and was a dependable, enthusiastic friend who arranged her joint custody schedule to match mine. To combat the stress of our divorces and single parenthood, we played and traveled together. Our friendship dramatically improved our quality of life and that of our children. Laura stepped up in a multitude of ways, adding sunshine during some very dark days.

My younger sister Kim moved from the west coast to Ohio after our mother died, so we could share our lives. She's been an equally important rock. I am so grateful for her! My relationship with Laura was different because we weren't family. It's also true of my best male friend at the time, BJ. It was deeply meaningful that these non-family members made themselves available to me. Between Laura, Kim, and BJ, I survived five brutal years in the legal system.

Constantly moving makes it harder to connect with caring people. Usually, these kinds of "anchors" are people with whom you've grown up, been through thick or thin, gone to college, or known for years. I have a few of them, but they don't live near me. We all want to have a sense of belonging and community where we live, a place where people "get" us, and are willing to help when they notice we're having a bad day.

Veterans don't take for granted the people who go the extra mile and demonstrate their love for us. That isn't unique to military people, but the need can be more piercing because of our lack of a civilian network and so many post-service losses.

4. Employers

Until recently, Servicemembers leaving the military received four or five days of civilian job search preparation. Many Veterans have never interviewed for a job nor written a resume and lack a community support network. They'll venture into the unstructured environment of American society that emphasizes rugged individualism, "every man for himself." They usually feel unprepared for this, like they're living in a foreign land. More than 90% report experiencing obstacles in obtaining civilian employment. My Veteran friends and I have experienced this directly.

Military candidates' resumes often contain excessive military terms; their desired job and career outcomes aren't always clear. Immersion in team-dominated culture limits their ability to self-promote and communicate qualities and experiences that make them the best individual for a position. Before the transition assistance program, most Veterans haven't heard of an "elevator pitch" and don't understand its value. Ultimately, the responsibility to prepare for post-military life rests with each Servicemember, but they are usually poorly prepared.

Civilians might ask, "Shouldn't they figure out who they are, what they're passionate about and which career to pursue? Can they access career and job-search services, and network? Do they ask for help, follow guidance, or utilize Veteran benefits? Are they willing to pay for needed gap services to reach their full potential?"

Many Veterans have done so and will continue to do so. But that isn't the norm. How many people do you know (military or civilian) who do all these things? A handful? Most of us need guidance and coaching to choose our best-fit career.

It takes nearly a year to transform a civilian into a military warrior. Without a similar investment to help them return to civilian life, over half feel disconnected from American society.

Coming from a highly structured environment impacts our ability to self-actualize. In the military, everything is clearly defined: what to wear, what to eat and where (if you're on base or deployed), who your friends can be, how to behave, do your job, develop subordinates, and how to advance professionally. This can be stifling if you like autonomy (like I do). But, this role clarity underpins why our Armed Forces are the most capable in the world, and why our military missions succeed.

Post-military, many Veterans experience a loss of identity, meaning, and purpose. If they've been to war, they may struggle with the loss of comrades, grief, survivor's guilt and/or PTSD, all of which complicates transition. This can extend to less than optimal investment in their career preparation, and job-search activities.

It takes time to recover from the price they paid defending our freedom. These unfortunate consequences of war earn our Veterans special consideration.

The Right Direction Despite Obstacles

For post 9/11 Veterans in the 2011 civilian labor market, unemployment was 12.1 percent. We've made much progress since then. Before the COVID-19 Pandemic, The Department of Labor reported in January 2020 that civilian unemployment rate was 3.4 percent. In comparison, Veteran unemployment rate was 3.1 percent across the nation; It was the seventeenth consecutive month that their unemployment rate was lower.

This groundswell is credited to civilian employers hiring Veterans in record numbers. Veteran Champion employers recognize that hiring Veterans is much more than corporate citizenship (social responsibility) or fulfilling diversity and inclusion initiatives. Most understand how Veterans strengthen their labor force, that it is a smart business decision and impacts the bottom line.

Research confirms these findings. According to The Society of Human Resource Management (SHRM) Foundation 68% of employers report that Veterans perform "better" or "much better" than civilian peers. An October 2017 Korn Ferry study of 1,000 executives found that while those surveyed appreciated the leadership, team and mission focus of Veterans, almost 70% said that there was no training for hiring managers on Veteran-specific hiring practices, and more than 60% said there was no onboarding or transition support for Veteran hires.

These are common employer objections regarding Servicemember applicants: Employer is troubled by preconceived, personal misconceptions or biases, candidate may have PTSD, or be too bossy; Applicant's behavior may be more formal than is comfortable, making them seem unapproachable; Employer may think they're odd; Despite having heard Servicemember's skills are highly transferrable and valuable, the employer is unsure how to leverage them; Concerns about applicant being a good fit with employees; They don't know the candidate.

Employers can easily overcome two common disconnects prospective military hires face. Many don't realize that 91% of military job classification codes have a direct civilian equivalent or how to translate a Military Occupational Specialty (MOS) code to the civilian workforce.

Without recruiters and hiring managers who can interpret and compare these skills with civilian KSAs (knowledge, skill and abilities) military job candidates feel they're speaking a foreign language.

Skills translators—the O*Net OnLine Military Crosswalk Search and the U.S. Department of Labor CareerOne Stop Civilian-to-Military Occupation Translator—make speaking the same language much easier.

In response to the 2020 COVID-19 pandemic, I envision Veterans to be in even greater demand (by informed employers) due to their ability to manage crisis, thrive in ambiguity and under pressure, agility, and team orientation. These "future-proof" leadership qualities second nature to Veterans are needed now more than ever.

What Insiders Know

Veteran Champion Employers understand the value of Veterans. They appreciate that military training shapes their thinking and behavior. Soft skills like work ethic, leadership, professionalism, adaptability, trainability, discipline, working well under pressure, and teamwork are stronger because of military service. Employers know that Veterans bring more productivity and less absenteeism; they're more mission-focused and more loyal. Veterans are entrepreneurial, comfortable working in highly diverse groups and are technologically savvy. Employers value their code of ethics, pursuit of excellence, integrity, and service before self.

Most importantly, these employers understand Veteran-hiring isn't charity work. Such an investment requires careful consideration to result in satisfying employment and retention of talent.

The "Veteran-Ready" employer is purposeful, proactive, metric driven and committed to Veteran-hiring over the long haul. They prepare for Veteran interviews differently than civilian ones. They use skills translators to align transferable military skills with civilian position KSAs. They know which questions to ask and which to avoid. During the interview they put Veterans at ease and get them talking. "Veteran-Ready" employers take pride in consistently making best-fit career matches. They offer specific onboarding, career advancement and engage Veteran employees in various ways, especially Veteran attraction, recruitment, interviewing and retention. They're interested in seeing the Veteran succeed because, when they do, everyone benefits. Hiring Veterans boosts a company's public image and helps them gain enormous customer goodwill.

Lauren Chess of Colonial Life and Accident Insurance Company says it best.

"Recruiting Veterans improves the organization's brand value and is the best way to say, 'Thank you' to the people who risked their lives for us."

The Veteran Champion Way

If both the hiring team and military job candidate knew how to connect and were better prepared, the military candidate would be more competitive and more likely to be chosen for the job. It's a huge step forward for an employer to be aware, proactive and take the lead in helping the relationship succeed. Veterans respond well to an employer's insightful leadership, which increases the employer's likelihood of hiring an employee with great potential.

Next begins the learning curve, for both the employer and Veteran. The employer learns to connect with, support, and leverage the Veteran's skill set to strengthen the company. The Veteran learns how to function and excel in environments with fewer boundaries, different social norms, and unfamiliar communication styles. That successful outcome is a powerful win-win!

I'm hopeful that in time, Veteran job candidates will be better equipped for the civilian job search process. The good news is that in 2012, former President Obama directed that the Transition Assistance Program be overhauled. The goal is to ensure Servicemembers are well prepared to compete for their chosen civilian career when they leave military service.

Who Should Take the Lead?

Currently, we're in the longest period of continuous war in our nation's history. Every year 200,000 Veterans separate from active duty!

Whose job is it to prepare those Servicemembers for post-military careers? Should the DOD shoulder this responsibility? Or should they focus on our national defense? Presently, they absorb most of the career coaching and job preparation responsibility. These programs are still in their infancy.

What about the VA? Is it their job to provide career coaching and job preparation? As a master's prepared R.N., my answer is a resounding "No!"

Their demanding, complex, and ever-evolving job is to provide the best possible healthcare to Veterans with service-connected disabilities. They can't be all things to all Veterans. And we don't want them to be.

I believe our best option is to fully engage the private sector, and cultivate employer Veteran Champions, who understand how to source, hire, and retain Veteran talent. They will benefit the most from this investment, strengthening their workforce as they improve the quality of life of our Veterans and their families.

Employer Veteran Champion Stories

Everyday business heroes go out of their way to do what it right for Veterans and by so doing, improve our workforce, communities, and many people's quality of life, not just the Veteran's. As the backbone of our economy, most jobs are generated by small-to medium-size businesses. They usually have fewer people and resources to invest in Veteran-hiring initiatives. And yet, many are doing this important work. Let's look at a few. I hope their stories inspire you like they have me.

Serving Veterans Serves Me

For Vice President of Marketing at Equitable Mortgage, Todd Reigle, serving those who've served our country is his greatest passion. It arose from Todd's love of history, his grandfather's military service during World War II, (though he never spoke of it) and getting to know Reserve Officer Training Corps (ROTC) cadets at the University of Rio Grande.

In college, Todd learned the value of community service. For years he's supported community causes that emphasized Veterans. He's been an Honor Flight Guardian nine times, served on Honor Flight Ground Crew seven times, participated for at least a decade in Wreaths Across America and volunteered three years on the Central Ohio Stand Down committee for homeless Veterans. As co-founder of Ohio Honor Ride, in two years he and Veteran friends cycled 600 miles raising $30,000 for Veteran organizations.

Through Adam's Hope Ministries, he donated goods and money for care packages mailed to deployed servicemen. While working at Goodwill Columbus, he co-hosted Veteran art therapy classes with the City of Columbus.

Todd is uniquely suited to serve Veterans because of his car accident-related PTSD in which three close friends' lives were lost.

"My service to Veterans helps me heal my own PTSD symptoms," Todd said.

Because his PTSD is not military related, he hopes sharing his coping experiences will benefit Veterans. Battling PTSD is a lifelong experience made easier by connecting with those who live full lives despite it.

Todd's biggest source of pride is thanking every Veteran he meets.

"A lot of these folks have never been thanked, so my goal is making sure they know at least one American is grateful for their service."

Grow Forward Gives Back

Anthony Redic is Managing Director and Chief Financial Officer of Grow Forward CFO, a small business providing strategic financial and operational support for small businesses. After getting acquainted at a business expo, I asked what he was doing to support Veterans. Despite the fact he was the son of an Air Force Veteran, he said he'd never thought about how he might be able to help.

I asked him, "Would you consider offering complimentary financial expertise to a small Veteran-owned business?" Immediately, he replied, "Of course!"

Two months later, he'd met with a Veteran small-business owner. Anthony committed to providing one year of support to help build capacity, generate free cash flow and enhance their balance sheet; Anthony's way of giving back to those that have done so much for us.

How Much Grace?

As the Managing Partner at SERVPRO in Delaware, Ohio, Leah Cottrill-Mescher has been hiring Veterans for about three years. Currently, they represent one third of her team.

"They get the job done, don't mind getting their hands dirty and like to help people. They have grit and know how to respond in crisis situations." Leah runs the family-owned and operated franchise specializing in cleaning mold, blood-borne pathogens, and disaster remediation after fire, flood, vandalism and more.

Leah is highly patriotic, pays well, offers benefits, and treats Veterans with respect. She's incredibly proud to support them inside and outside the company. Realizing that "hero worship" makes Servicemembers feel uncomfortable, she tries to "keep it casual."

She appreciates their mission focus. A few years back, her team was offered the opportunity to travel to Florida and assist with Hurricane Michael cleanup. Veterans were the first to volunteer, and they did so over the Thanksgiving holiday.

Leah is a soft-hearted, mild-mannered woman who sometimes found it challenging to communicate with Veteran team members. Their direct and sometimes authoritative demeanor and communication style occasionally made her uncomfortable. She also worried their approach might negatively affect clients during disaster remediation, often emotionally laden.

For one key staff member, she hired a male professional-growth coach to help him develop a different communication style. The coaching was a success and improved co-management between herself and other members of the civilian management team. This Veteran leader subsequently coached other Veteran staff members helping them develop closer working relationships with management.

On another occasion, a new Veteran hire exhibited unexpected difficult behaviors. She wanted to know, "How much grace do I offer?"

"It's important to state work and behavior expectations and emphasize that inappropriate behavior has consequences," I said. "Hiring Veterans isn't charity work."

Veterans usually respond well to a direct approach. In turn, they must come to work prepared to be productive, professional, and ready to perform the mission! When needed, Servicemembers need to be encouraged to use Employee Assistance Programs, community

Veteran support resources, and take personal responsibility.

Leah hired Vanguard Veteran to brand her company as Veteran-Friendly through social media posting and meeting Veterans. By attending community round tables and other events, she learned firsthand what it's like to transition from the military to civilian life. She understands how important it is to hear their stories and build trusting relationships.

"I'm truly proud of what they do for our country and every day in our business. They bring such depth, higher level of caring, and intelligence to our team. They're incredible people who just want the chance to 'come home' and live the life they fought so hard to give each one of us. It's my honor to support them."

Because SERVPRO across the nation understands how Servicemembers strengthen the workforce, they're investing in a nationwide Veteran-hiring program.

Taking Care of Those Who Take Care of Us

Founded in 1995 by Bruce Calabrese, Equitable Mortgage Corporation is solely dedicated to bringing back client satisfaction and changing the way home buying, lending, and home refinancing is perceived. The company has provided over six billion in residential loans, serving loans from $50,000 to $5,000,000 and assisting thousands of clients in ten states.

At a military job fair in 2018, President Tony Butler hired their first Servicemember, an Air Force Veteran with no lending experience. Tony was confident in his choice because he knew that Veterans:

- Know how to follow policy and procedures.
- Are trustworthy, disciplined and easily inspire trust in clients.
- Emphasize teamwork and complete the mission.

To help distinguish Equitable Mortgage as Veteran-Friendly, they placed a patriotic wrap on their company van and have a LoansThatHonor notification on their website. Bruce and his team attend local Veteran community events to build relationships and cultivate a grassroots talent pipeline.

They feel a responsibility to support Veteran causes and do so in many ways. Bruce Calabrese inspires his team to "Take care of those who take care of us." His son, a key firm executive, is a certified Veteran Loan specialist. For every VA loan they close, they donate $500 to Columbus Honor Flight—to date they've donated $23,000. To expand their reach and brand the company Veteran-Friendly they hired Mr. Todd Reigle. They support Veterans by making financial contributions to Adaptive Sports Connection Water Sports Weekend, Marine Corps Family Support Community, the 121st Air Refueling Wing at Rickenbacker Air National Guard Base and the QFM 96 Red, White and Q Fund. They sponsored and attended Vanguard Veteran's Inaugural "Veteran-Ready" Employer Introduction training.

Currently, about 7.5% of their employees are Veterans. Their family-oriented, "take care of each other" culture and sincerely listening to what Veterans have to say promotes successful post-military transition and retention. They're just beginning their journey and are confident that as Equitable grows, the Veteran presence will also.

Honor and Serve Veterans in Life and Death

Michael Schoedinger is the sixth-generation owner and President of Schoedinger Funeral and

Cremation Service in Columbus, Ohio. Although no family members served and he's not a Veteran himself, he's passionate about honoring and serving them in life and in death.

I met Mike when he participated and championed the employer-focused community relations program at the 121st Air Refueling Wing at Rickenbacker Air National Guard Base in Columbus, Ohio.

In response to 9/11, I led the creation of this mission-critical initiative per the direction of Wing Commander Brigadier General A.J. Feucht and the guidance of Vice Wing Commander Colonel Robert L. Boggs. We hosted military immersion experiences (observing an in-air refueling onboard a KC-135 "Tanker") twice a month to foster understanding and build relationships with civilians, emphasizing employers. After Mike's flight, I asked if he'd be willing to help us identify other employers to invite. He was very generous.

As Ohio's largest, family-owned funeral home, Schoedinger is a Veteran-Friendly employer, hiring numerous Servicemembers over their 165-year history. Operating fifteen locations, and managing hundreds of Veteran funerals each year, they ensure Veterans receive the tribute they deserve.

Schoedinger has been the exclusive local partner of Veterans Funeral and Memorial Care since its founding. They offer special benefits and discount Veteran funeral services. They're the only local partner of Cell Phones for Soldiers, recycling used phones free to Veterans.

In 2004 Mike brought the Vietnam Wall traveling memorial to Central Ohio. His visionary leadership resulted in an outpouring of community donations and more than 75,000 visitors: ten times the usual turnout. Over 300 volunteers were recruited for the 24 hour/3-day weekend event.

In December 2007, Schoedinger brought Wreaths Across America to Central Ohio for the first time, mirroring Arlington National Cemetery's tribute. Over 3,000 wreaths were placed on Veterans' graves throughout Greenlawn Cemetery and Kingwood Memorial Park.

"Without the support of the community, we wouldn't have been able to do that," Mike said. "Two dollars of every $15 wreath purchase went to Ohio Civil Air Patrol. Hundreds of volunteers unloaded wreaths from trucks and placed them on graves. Then, God blessed us with snow. Green wreaths with red bows lay on the white snow of each grave. The beautiful result was so stunning it made the front page of the Columbus Dispatch on Sunday morning!"

As a member and past President of Columbus Rotary, Mike brought numerous Veteran speakers to weekly programs. The club established a committee to partner Rotarian business leaders with Ohio State University Veteran students to provide mentoring as they transition from college to the civilian workforce.

Most recently, Schoedinger partnered with Honor Flight Columbus recruiting Veterans, guardians, and sponsors. He joined the board and through his media connections, leveraged thousands of dollars of sponsorships, free public service announcements, television, and radio commercials.

"I don't cry very often, but every time I hear a 21-gun salute and Taps played at a funeral, I get emotional; even when I didn't know the deceased. Seeing smiles on Veterans faces at events makes me smile. To get a hug instead of a handshake at the grave after a funeral warms my heart.

The best was during the Vietnam Wall Experience when numerous wives, daughters, and friends of Vietnam Veterans came to me and said through tears, 'Thank you! My husband hasn't talked about his time in the war in forty years. He opened up to me last night and shared things he's had bottled up for decades.'"

Michael has been extraordinarily patriotic since he was a little boy. As an adult, he's a pioneer and an influential Veteran Champion role model. He broadens awareness in the business community about the value of hiring Veterans.

When asked how to become a Veteran Champion, Mike says, "Start small. Ask a Veteran you know what 'alumni' activities they're involved in. Call a local Veterans of Foreign Wars (VFW) or American Legion and ask their leaders where help is needed. Talk to your employer to see what they've done in the past, and what resources they're willing to commit to future endeavors."

Veteran-Friendly is a Process

Buckeye Power Sales' (BPS) Human Resource (HR) Director Susan Malaby, has strong ties to the military. Her father is an army Veteran, several great-uncles served, and a cousin served in Vietnam; even the brother of Susan's assistant is a Veteran.

This patriotic, family-owned business expects employees to live by a set of core values and military personnel have most if not all of them. BPS values their service and shows support by actively recruiting Servicemembers. Of their 200 plus employees, nearly 12% are Veterans.

BPS recognized early on the limited number of applicants with generator knowledge. The Armed Forces became one of their few resources. The HR director's first step was attending a webinar through Monster.com which outlined how employers can help transitioning Servicemembers. This fostered a better understanding of the challenges Veterans face post-service. She then held a recruiting event with a service manager in Indianapolis.

"We then partnered with a firm that focuses on military placement. In 2019 our recruiter went to a seminar held by Vanguard Veteran and came back very enthusiastic! This reenergized our efforts."

Military personnel with generator experience and mechanical ability fit BPS well because they're used to working in inclement weather, are physically able to do the job, and can work under stress. The company benefited when they identified a military source for hard-to-find candidates and hired qualified talent able to quickly ramp-up and contribute.

Their technicians make a very comfortable living. Because BPS is experienced hiring former and active military personnel, they know what it takes to transfer KSAs, acclimate them and help them build a successful career. BPS offers a full range of benefits, including an Employee Assistance Program and other voluntary benefits because some of their former Servicemembers dealt with PTSD. Susan emphasizes the importance of having adequate benefits.

They provide a good work/life balance including paid time off and formal training to help them advance in their career.

BPS has been in business since 1947. They have formal, documented growth plans, which provides stability and opportunities for their employees.

To date they:

- Offer a discount to Servicemembers every day
- Celebrate Veteran's Day at each of their seven locations which includes a breakfast for all employees with recognition of Servicemember and Veteran employees
- Recognize Veterans in company correspondence

- Donated a generator for a home built by Building for Americas Bravest for a disabled Veteran

"I'm so proud to work for a company that embraces supporting our Armed Forces. I'm talking to leadership about next steps so we can truly boast being a Veteran-Friendly company. Ideas include food and clothing drives, packing care boxes, or holding a fundraiser."

Being a true Veteran-Friendly company is a process, it doesn't happen overnight. Companies must decide the "what and why" behind their efforts, and the level of available resources. Despite limited resources, BPS found ways to expand their programs.

Susan recommends partnering with people and agencies who are excited to work with you! Military personnel come with built-in KSA's and core values that benefit your company.

"Learn some of the military lingo—it makes communication easier!"

City-wide Veteran Appreciation

Central Ohio Transit Authority (COTA) is dedicated to improving mobility. Headquartered in Columbus, Ohio, COTA ensures economic and social affluence for the region by connecting people to prosperity through the removal of mobility barriers.

Dedicated to improving the lives of local Veterans and active military, COTA has more than 1,200 employees; 12% are Veterans. COTA President/CEO, Joanna M. Pinkerton is proud to serve Veterans. Pinkerton views serving as the top executive at COTA an opportunity to give back to the Veteran community, which has been a large part of her personal and professional life. Her father is a Purple Heart recipient from the Vietnam war. Both grandfathers volunteered for WWII but were denied military service because their occupations—a coal miner and railroader—were considered essential in supporting the home front war effort.

In April 2018, one of Joanna's priorities was establishing their first Veteran Employee Resource Group (VERG). Their goals included: Giving a voice to Veteran employees and Veteran advocates; Strengthening COTA's Veteran work force; Retaining talent; Attracting Veteran employee candidates; Participating in meaningful and beneficial local Veteran causes.

Jana Davis, COTA's Diversity and EEO Administrator, led the launch of VERG and established their Veteran-hiring program. Jana's father served in the Air Force during the Korean War. Through her previous career in workforce development, Jana worked closely with Veterans, assisting in their career placement. It is Jana's passion to show her appreciation for and support Veterans.

Jana established COTA's Veteran-Friendly brand by attending career fairs at the Columbus VA, Congressman Stivers' Veteran Job Fair, the Human Resources of Central Ohio Veteran Job Fair at Cardinal Health, and other events. She connected with Veteran Community influencers, including the Ohio Department of Veterans Services, and local Veteran community organization leaders. She tirelessly cultivates relationships with Veterans. Jana's email signature block includes the mantra, "Thank a Vet. Hire a Vet. Admire a Vet."

After supporting the launch, Janna delegated leadership of the VERG to its members. They chose the name, logo, and community service projects. By a majority vote, VERG members selected this purpose statement: "The VERG is committed to serving the employees of COTA and Community Partners through innovative and diverse initiatives, programs and activities. Members of VERG strive to provide an inclusive environment and advocate for the growth, career advancement and overall support of all COTA's employees and their families."

The VERG prioritizes community involvement. Some examples include supporting the National Veterans Memorial and Museum, Habitat for Humanity, and the United States Marine Corps Toys for Tots.

Jana recruits Veterans using these best practices:

- Inviting Veteran employees to assist at job fairs
- Including Veterans in the interview process
- Spearheading a Veteran-specific onboarding
- Highlighting COTA's commitment to Veteran hiring on the COTA Careers web page
- Coaching Veteran candidates to align their strengths with job choices and how to navigate the job application process
- Assisting Veterans with the COTA Careers application, resume writing, and interviewing skills

Every year COTA hosts a pre-Veteran's Day breakfast to thank more than one-hundred employees who have served our country. When Joanna asked VERG to elevate the previous celebration, the group created a color guard to open the event. Led by somber bagpipe music, the guard presented the colors for the first time, a moving experience for all.

After breakfast, Servicemembers boarded a Veteran-branded bus, adorned with a patriotic wrap reading "Proud to honor our employees who served and continue to serve." The electronic message across the front of the bus flashed, "Thank You Veterans." That week, all three-hundred-twenty of their transit fleet carried the message. Veterans were transported downtown to walk in the annual Columbus Veteran's Parade, while dozens of COTA employees cheered and waved American flags to honor their coworkers.

Guard Members Start Nationwide Company

Being a Veteran Champion employer has been part of Schneider Trucking since its inception. Bill Buechel, Director of Schneider Trucking's Military Program, stated that efforts to recruit from the military began in 1935. Company founder, Al Schneider, was a National Guardsman. He recruited fellow Guard members as his first employees. Of their 15,650 employees nationwide, approximately 15% are Veterans.

Successful Veteran hiring starts with their interaction with their recruiting team. They have recruiters who specialize in understanding the company's military benefits, GI Bill benefits and converting military experience into civilian pay. Schneider has conducted application reviews on a SATCOM phone from Iraq and talked to candidates still in South Korea preparing for their post-military career. They do Facebook Live events, with military-specific video success stories.

From a driver perspective, the metrics that guide their hiring success is evaluating each candidate's eligibility independently.

They also have a team of Veterans with which current and former military personnel can work throughout their transition. Schneider offers a Military Apprenticeship Program, where Veterans earn up to $1,431 per month their first year with Schneider (above and beyond their Schneider paycheck.)

To retain military talent, they work to understand what the Veteran wants in their career and tries to find their "best-fit" match. Once hired, they emphasize maximizing Veteran employee skillsets. Schneider offers a competitive and civilian equivalent driver pay package based on the Veteran's time in the military.

For over eighty years, they've developed best practices. Their core values are safety, integrity, respect, and excellence and is the basis of how the business operates. This philosophy is easily transferable to former and current military personnel.

Schneider understands the commitment and sacrifice required to support a Servicemember's obligations to the Guard and Reserve. Associates are not obligated to take vacation time to attend drill or Annual Training.

Schneider is honored to be one of the first employers to join the Wounded Warrior Program.

Some of their Veteran-hiring awards include:
- Presented the first-ever Secretary of Defense Employer Support Freedom Award
- First to be named Supportive Employer of the Guard and Reserves by The Enlisted Association of the National Guard of the United States. This annual award is named after the company founder: The Al Schneider Memorial Award

- Ranked #6 on Best Company for Veterans by Monster and Military.com
- Named Most Valuable Employer (MVE) by RecruitMilitary
- Top Veteran-Friendly Company by U.S. Veterans Magazine

Schneider's fleets of eleven *Ride of Pride* trucks are designed to be rolling tributes to members of the military. Each is captained by an elite Schneider driver with military experience.

This fleet participates in events such as Wreaths Across America and other military-themed events.

"Military families are strong and resilient," Bill said. "There may be occasions when, due to military service, they are separated from each other. During that time, Schneider ensures requirements and expectations are communicated. The company continues benefits and differential pay if the Veteran is deployed for up to eighteen months."

Due to the density of current and former military personnel working at Schneider, one of our most valuable resources is an active Veteran network on which associates and their spouses rely.

"Hiring and retaining Veterans is the right thing to do!" Bill said. "Servicemembers bring a unique commitment and skillset that allows them to prosper in career opportunities at Schneider."

He offers these practical tips for employers interested in hiring and retaining Veterans:

- Encourage Veterans to interact with job candidates—to be the face of the company.
- Invest in Veteran-specific programs that attract and retain this talent.
- Share your military success stories internally and externally.
- Rely on Veteran associates to be company advocates.

These are stories from just a few of many Veteran Champions. Employers across the nation are inspiring each other with innovations that advance Veteran hiring and retention.

Large corporations actively hire Veterans. For example, the Boeing Company prioritizes Veteran hiring and retention, creating best practices for others to follow. Cardinal Health and Nationwide are examples of companies who've received the Secretary of Defense Employer Support of Guard and Reserve Freedom Award, a prestigious acknowledgment earned by only fifteen employers across the nation annually who excel at hiring Servicemembers.

In 2011, JP Morgan Chase began the 100,000 Jobs Mission with ten leading companies committed to hiring 100,000 Veterans by 2020, surpassing it in 2014. Now with more than 200 companies from nearly every industry, renamed Veteran Jobs Mission, their hiring goal is 1,000,000. As of early 2020, more than 565,700 Servicemembers have been hired.

5. The Faith Community

Freedom is not free; it comes at a price. Veterans pay the price physically and in unseen, spiritual ways. Their families feel it, too. Warriors may experience moral injury, soul injury, and other emotional injuries—especially those who have directly fought in or supported combat operations. These kinds of injuries may cause warriors to feel cut off from God and from themselves.

Of the 2.6 million post-9/11 era Veterans, about 40% find it difficult to find meaning or purpose in life and have lost touch with their spirituality or religion. Over half feel disconnected from civilian life; one-quarter to one-half may have trouble making new friends, getting involved in their communities, and finding or keeping a job.

Spirituality—that which gives purpose and meaning to life—is found in relationships with God, a higher power, self, others, and nature. It is an essential element in understanding the nature, effects of and recovery from traumatic experiences. Crisis, no matter what its source, is always a spiritual crisis because it involves the destruction of meaning. For these reasons, the faith community has a special and unique role.

Dr. Bruce Norman, a Navy Vietnam Veteran bereavement counselor with a PhD in theology, believes everything that affects Veterans is spiritual in nature.

"Veteran issues are less related to a particular medical intervention," he says, "and more a part of their personal spiritual journey towards perspective, meaning, and healing."

To engage clergy, in 2010, the U.S. Department of Veterans Affairs Office of Rural Health and the National VA Chaplain Center created the Community Clergy Training Program (CCTP). Its purpose is to educate faith communities about how to better utilize resources to support Veterans and their families, especially those who feel alienated, isolated, or helpless. It sensitizes them to support those left behind when a Servicemember deploys to war. To help Veteran's and their families prepare, endure, and reestablish after deployment, and after separating from active duty service. And, help Veterans get in touch with their spirituality.

Our military is now an all-volunteer force, including those serving full-time on active status. Prior to 9/11, Guard and Reserve members historically participated in "drill" training one weekend a month and annual training two consecutive weeks per year. In those days, the chance of being mobilized to active duty to support areas of conflict was low. Most military members don't want to be in combat, but they welcome the opportunity to use their training and perform their job. After 9/11, Reserve and Guard members got this opportunity. Their chances of being deployed rose to nearly eighty percent.

In 2009, I had the opportunity to design, lead and execute a never-been-done-before state-wide outreach office for the Ohio National Guard. In response to 9/11, our mission was to educate and engage civilians in support of troops and their families. Why was this important? Because Guard and Reserve members were deploying in a way our nation had never experienced, increasing their needs and the needs of their families. Our charge was to inspire and guide our citizenry to help meet these needs.

As the commander of the Ohio National Guard (or The Adjutant General) it was Major General Gregory L. Wayt's vision to mobilize Ohio's citizenry through the outreach office. Realizing his intent was the crowning achievement of my military career. We accomplished the mission by inviting civilian influencers to one-day military immersion experiences and engaging them in military-civilian coalitions. Through them, we cultivated mutually beneficial activities, services, and resources to meet the needs of Servicemembers and their families.

Neither the DOD, nor VA can meet all the needs of our warriors. And they shouldn't, not just because they will never have enough resources, but because every citizen has a stake in it. Helping Servicemembers and Military Connected Families through deployments and adjusting to civilian life post-service is everyone's business! Every citizen has an opportunity—if not an obligation—to do their part and "be a part of the win."

In the fifth year of the outreach office, Margaret called me from Northern Ohio.

"We've been trying to engage clergy because our military families need the support of the faith community. I mailed two-hundred letters to clergy leaders and got no response. Can you help?" Through this phone call and a recent presentation on moral injury (damage to one's moral conscience and values), I heard God telling me to act.

Two other milestone events launched the clergy outreach initiative. Retired Navy Chaplain Carla Cherry, from the Chalmers P. Wylie VA Ambulatory Care Clinic, invited me, Ohio Army National Guard State Chaplain Colonel

Andrew Aquino and Ohio Air National Guard Wing Chaplain Lt. Col. Curtiss Wagner to a webinar, hosted by the Department of Veterans Affairs National VA Chaplain Center. This introduction and a nudge from Joe Schrock, a retired active Army Chaplain, and Senior Pastor at Zion Evangelical Lutheran Church in Hamilton, Ohio jump-started the Guard's clergy outreach.

After the Southern Ohio Synod of the Evangelical Lutheran Church in America held the CCTP, Pastor Schrock called to ask, "Why isn't the Ohio National Guard hosting this training?"

"Great idea! We should," I replied. That was it... we were on our way.

Ohio's New Clergy Initiative

Nearly 300 Ohio clergy participated in the two-day CCTP training. Some returned to their communities to teach the course to peers, others provided more meaningful support for military families in their congregations. Forty pastors agreed to serve as advisers for faith community leaders starting military ministries. The Clergy Working Group hosted quarterly meetings to cultivate and expand best practices and created the Military Ministry Tool Kit.

Clergy are busy, un-resourced, overworked, underpaid and participation in faith communities is declining. Meaning, they must do more with less and don't have time to organize and lead these ministries themselves.

That's why after my military retirement, Lt. Col. Joe Machado, a retired Army Vietnam Veteran, and I founded the nonprofit Veteran Interfaith Bridge. Our mission is to inspire and equip volunteer faith community leaders to start military ministries. The goal isn't to create therapists or counselors, but kind-hearted, hospitable, and informed citizens willing to build trusting relationships, who are sincere about meeting the needs of Servicemembers and their families. And when it is needed, they know how and where to refer them for additional care.

CCTP trains clergy, Veteran Interfaith Bridge trains volunteers to work in partnership with clergy. Volunteers rooted in their spiritual beliefs, who love the military and are willing to pull Veterans together to help improve their quality of life. Such leaders could be a military spouse, child, or sibling; someone who knows or has helped a struggling Veteran and wants to give back. Or, anyone who cares about what happens to our Servicemembers.

If it works for you, start with prayer. Follow up by doing small practical acts of kindness such as: hosting a potluck; bringing a meal to someone who's ill; mowing the lawn for someone who's deployed; picking up something from the grocery store; participating in carpools. Invite a newly returned Veteran to one of the following: your place of worship; to join your book club; attend a parent teacher organization or civic club meeting. Invite the Servicemember or spouse to coffee and get to know them. Actively listen to their experiences. As trust develops, Veteran Champions may learn what troubles them. Veteran Champions connect with and reliably provide support. This isn't rocket science, it's people science.

Being a Veteran Champion is a Daily Conversation

Reverend Elizabeth Krall pastors the Perry United Methodist Church in Perry, Ohio. She's ministered for almost thirty years. As of this writing, she has influenced at least twenty clergy to start or expand military ministries. Krall has conversations everyday with pastors and lay people about what they can do and how to connect Veterans with community resources.

Having never served in the Military, she became aware of the need to get involved when she experienced friends and family who struggled with PTSD post-service.

She caught the "fire in her belly" in 2016 after participating in Ohio National Guard Clergy outreach and attending the CCTP. She's been a passionate Veteran Champion since, teaching CCTP to faith community leaders as often as possible.

"The CCTP is an extremely important training that all churches pastors & laity, need to be involved in," Reverend Krall said.

Some of her encounters with struggling Veterans and First Responders led to the development of strong grief support groups. She also shared her testimony in 2017 at the Opus Peace/Vanguard Veteran Fallen Comrades Ceremony at Trinity United Methodist Church in Columbus, Ohio.

Despite being a clergy member, Veterans of her own family were reluctant to accept her help. Instead, she suggested counseling through local agencies and kept encouraging them to pursue it. Unfortunately, only after a threatened suicide and divorce, did they finally seek help.

Veteran stoicism is common. Don't feel bad if your family member doesn't let you help. It's hard for loved ones to understand and to know how to deal with it. Do what she did, identify community Veteran support resources and keep encouraging your Veteran to use them.

Prayer and Pairing

"Let Veterans and their families know that you really care for them; that's what we are asked to do by God. Love your neighbor. It's just that simple."

Deacon Todd Tucky, with St. Mary's Catholic Church in Delaware, Ohio, identifies with Veterans who serve, because of his own call to the Diaconate. The word deacon means "To Serve." While Todd didn't serve in the military, his grandfather, father, and uncles did.

We met in 2014, through the Clergy Working Group. Whatever the outreach office offered clergy, he attended. He soaked it all up. One day, he called to ask if he could obtain additional education for supporting Veterans through formal education or other certifications. I wasn't aware of anything else.

"What else do I need to know or do before I start a military ministry?"

"Deacon, I think you've participated in everything the Guard has to offer," I said. "My friend, you have everything you need. Lead with your heart." That's my advice to anyone who truly wants to be a Veteran Champion: Lead with your heart. This is especially important within the faith community.

Catholic Deacons are ordained servant leaders who wear the collar, and voluntarily dedicate their lives to serving the church. Their job is to be "in the world" as Deacon Tucky puts it. Within those parameters, he built a regional nondenominational military ministry for the community at his church, founded on prayer and pairing with Veteran community mentors from the same branch of service. Regardless of their denomination, he starts with prayer. He believes that the most important first step is helping individuals build a prayer life. He then connects the Veteran seeking support with those who are doing well post-service.

This pairing works wonders. It's easier for Veterans to connect and walk shoulder to shoulder together. Even if it's just two brief conversations, it helps the Veteran feel like, "At least someone in my town gets me." This simple and powerful combination of prayer and pairing brings tears to my eyes because of how well it works. This is a huge support for a Veteran feeling confused, lost, and alone.

Todd isn't a behavioral health provider; he owns a computer business. As a Deacon, he's trained how to support hurting people, and when to refer someone, but he had no experience supporting Veterans. Several years ago, Todd had uncertainties about supporting Veterans because of what he'd heard about PTSD and suicide. Since starting his military ministry, I asked about his experiences with these concerns.

"You know," he said, "It's never come up."

I contend that because the Veteran connected with a person of faith and a "same service" Veteran who cared about them, lifelines were formed. This support grounded the transitioning Veteran in their adjustment to civilian life. When Veterans adapt well and begin their spiritual healing, they're much better able to support their family and contribute to their community. That's a win-win!

Deacon Tucky shares these important tips:

- This is a ministry of presence. Simply be there for someone. All you need to do is show up. Sometimes that's enough.

- We are all equipped to help, if even just to listen, hold their hand, let them know they're valued and loved.
- You're not alone. There are many resources to help and support anyone thinking about this ministry. There's an old saying, "If you want to go fast, go alone. If you want to go far, go together"
- The best way to help deployed Servicemembers, is helping their family with day-to-day and unexpected things e.g., car repairs or the air conditioner going out.

Deacon Tucky champions the needs of Veterans in additional ways. He trains deacons in the Catholic Diocese of Columbus how to start military ministries and is having conversations with the Cleveland and Cincinnati Dioceses and seminaries about how to expand understandings and engagement of deacons in military ministry.

"Veterans aren't 'special snowflakes,' who do what they do for glory or recognition." he said. "They [act] out of a genuine love of neighbor and sense of duty. They put everything aside for others. How can one not want to help and support them in any way possible?"

Don't Wait for a Tragedy

Pastor Jeff Beckley is the Associate Pastor in Youth and Family at Memorial Baptist Church in Columbus, Ohio. Although he had been introduced to the idea of military ministry through the Guard's Clergy outreach program, a tragedy made it personal and woke up his church. On November 24, 2014, twenty-seven-year old church member Army Specialist Joseph W. Riley was killed in action from wounds suffered in a vehicle-borne Improvised Explosive Device (IED) in Afghanistan.

"This was hard on all of us in the church," he said. "He grew up in the church, was beloved by all, and his parents are our music directors." Pastor Beckley was especially concerned about Mr. Riley to whom he paid careful attention. He watched as the father mourned his loss by serving Veterans. This experience reinforced in Jeff the unique role of the faith community and the meaningful opportunities to serve Military Connected Families. He wanted to learn and do more.

"We loved our military families before this tragedy. The difference is that now we want to find ways to show them our love."

He championed the father's efforts to support Veterans. Together they gave the benediction and remarks at the Wounded Warrior Amputee Softball Tournament. It was a powerful moment when Pastor Beckley and other church members shook their hands honoring these military heroes.

The military ministry at Memorial Baptist Church currently looks like this:

- Recognition of Veteran church members during military holidays
- Letters and care packages sent to active Servicemembers
- Send-off parties for active duty military members
- Counseling for individuals and families
- Looking for opportunities to provide transportation and other practical support for military families with deployed loved ones
- The Riley family informing them about ways to minister to military families

About five years later, Pastor Beckley reached out to me.

"Kathy, how do I connect with Veteran community services and area Veterans? We want to offer services from our coffee shop?"

"Jeff, if you want to do this, you have to get the VA involved." I connected him to the Columbus VA Chaplain to determine whether they could offer services onsite and encouraged him to contact the Franklin County Veteran Service Commission to explore opportunities.

Through their partnership with Jordan's Crossing, a ministry that helps addicts and homeless on the West side of Columbus, they found a location for the coffee shop. The church hopes this will be a lifeline for those in need, and Veterans in particular.

Pastor Beckley offers this advice to faith community leaders starting military ministries:

- Connect with organizations like Veteran Interfaith Bridge to learn how to approach and identify Veteran community resources
- Meet with other clergy that have done it, ask questions and get advice
- Talk to Veterans and those who love them in your congregation to gauge interest in leading a military ministry in your place of worship

"A young man who gave his life in service to others woke up our church to the needs of Servicemembers. May you and I continue honoring Specialist Joseph Riley's legacy by finding ways to help our men and women who risk their lives for our freedom."

6. The Legal Community

Operation Legal Help Ohio (OLHO), was a nonprofit started in 2013 by a team of ingenious legal minds: former Ohio Supreme Court Justice Evelyn Lundberg Stratton and Colonel Duncan Auckland, Chief Legal Counsel for the Ohio Adjutant General's Department. I worked alongside these visionary leaders through the Ohio National Guard's outreach office (hosting military immersion events) to help them attract volunteer attorneys to serve Veterans. Their mission was to provide civil legal case support for eligible active duty or low-income Veterans to avoid homelessness, remove employment barriers and protect health. These services included: rental conditions, eviction and foreclosure defense, driver's license reinstatement, and much more. Community organizations like this provide legal services that the VA cannot.

Civilian and military advocacy groups across the state joined to bridge "The Justice Gap," the unmet civil legal needs of Veterans. OLHO recruited, trained, and supported nearly 500 volunteer attorneys and represented Veterans at no charge. At VA facilities, they worked with Veterans at monthly, brief advice clinics and partnered with criminal defense attorneys and Veteran Treatment Courts (VTC).

Across the nation, there are over 400 VTC—a hybrid of drug courts and mental health courts—that emphasize treatment and diversion rather than punishment. It doesn't excuse Veteran defendants from their crime. Instead, it addresses underlying reasons potentially connected to their military service, and links them to resources that will most likely prevent repeat criminal behavior.

Active duty, Guard and Reserve members, and Veterans may participate if they meet eligibility criteria and are willing to commit to a rigorous twelve-to eighteen-month program. It requires frequent court appearances and mandatory attendance at treatment sessions. VTC usually have stricter probationary periods than traditional courts, including random drug and alcohol testing. Participants are assigned Veteran peer mentors, a critical part of the recovery process. The result is high program graduation rates and recidivism rates far below the national average.

Veterans who have met certain criteria and successfully complete treatment plans, may avoid jail or prison terms or have their charges dismissed. It's a beautiful thing!

Once OLHO considered its goal accomplished, they folded operations into more robust legal assistance programs, thanks to additional funding provided by the Ohio General Assembly to legal aid organizations. In addition, the Ohio State Bar Association Military and Veterans Affairs Committee and the Ohio Attorney General Veterans Courts and Military Affairs Subcommittee continue their strong advocacy efforts. Across Ohio, countless attorneys now provide pro bono assistance. I speak on behalf of all Ohio Veterans when I offer these Veteran Champions a sincere and heartfelt "Thank you!"

The Ultimate Veteran Champion Collaborator

Justice Evelyn Stratton never served in the military, but her family lineage included many who did. As part of a missionary family, she grew up living overseas in Thailand.

She served sixteen years as a justice on the Supreme Court of Ohio and seven years as a trial judge in the Court of Common Pleas. Throughout her career, she's championed mental health awareness, led collaborative efforts, and influenced many public policy solutions. In 2001, she formed and chaired the Supreme Court of Ohio Advisory Committee on Mental Illness and the Courts. They helped establish forty-five mental health courts, recommended changes to Medicaid and advocated for a new Juvenile Competency Statute.

Currently she leads, "Stepping Up, Ohio" part of a national initiative to reduce the incarceration of people with mental illness. A collaboration masterpiece, this initiative brings together a diverse cross section of legal professionals, service providers, state and local agencies, and other stakeholders. As of January 2019, forty-eight Ohio counties have passed resolutions supporting Stepping Up Ohio.

Before 2005, Justice Stratton noticed the needs of Veterans with PTSD and Traumatic Brain Injury (TBI) who were involved in the criminal justice system. She decided to do something about it.

"A Veteran is someone who gives the government a blank check, up to and including their life, to serve their country," Justice Stratton said. "We need to help our Veterans reclaim their lives and dignity. It is the least we can do to thank and support them upon their return."

She created many influential collaboratives that expanded legal and other services for Veterans in Ohio and across the nation. She worked on, established, led, or championed the development of these organizations, programs, and guidelines:

- The U.S. Department of Veterans Affairs criteria for creating VTC and the Veterans Justice Outreach program
- The Ohio Attorney General's Task Force on Criminal Justice and Mental Illness and the Veterans Court & Military Affairs subcommittee
- The Ohio State Bar Association Military and Veterans Affairs committee
- The establishment of VTC across Ohio
- Four statewide conferences for legal and other Veteran supporters
- The Resurrecting Lives Foundation, assisting Veterans with Traumatic Brain Injuries
- The Veteran Treatment Court Peer Mentor Guide
- Recommendations for judges who appoint Veterans' Service Commissioners

Justice Stratton's commitment to excellence and her ability to build effective grassroots coalitions gets things done. As a passionate and charismatic leader, she listens, encourages, recognizes the contributions of others and empowers them. She improves communities and quality of life by bringing citizens and people of great influence together and engaging them.

To become a legal Veteran Champion she offers these suggestions:

- Find and connect with the Veteran Justice Outreach coordinator in your territory.
- Find a judge willing to influence improvements in the criminal justice system in support of Veterans.
- Leverage local bar associations and Veteran's associations to help you advocate.
- Raise awareness about VTC.

"I love helping Veterans," she said. "But Justice Sharon Kennedy's leadership on their behalf, leaves me in the dust."

Make the Invisible, Visible

Ohio Supreme Court Justice Sharon Kennedy believes when Veterans enter the legal system, many hide or don't reveal their military service because they feel ashamed, fear the judge, or—if they didn't fight in active combat—may not consider themselves a Veteran. Those who suffer from PTSD or TBI may end up in criminal courts charged with drunken driving, domestic violence or starting bar fights. The Veteran and criminal justice systems often forget to consider and link consequences of military service to this behavior.

Because Justice Kennedy's career began as a police officer, she relates to and is particularly sensitive to the stressors of military service. According to the Supreme Court of Ohio website, "From the routine, to the heart-pounding, to the heart-breaking, she has seen it all."

This Veteran Champion is committed to making "the invisible, visible" and creating a seamless criminal justice system for Veterans. She travels across the state explaining to community members, elected officials, law enforcement, judges, attorneys, and mental health advocates, that many Veterans in the system don't receive the care they need. Justice Kennedy actively encourages judges to develop more VTC because of their high success rates.

She asks judges and police departments to cooperate in identifying Veterans in the jail system. Ohio recently passed a law requiring every judge to review a defendant's military background and whether it may be a mitigating factor in sentencing.

Building on work begun by Justice Stratton, Justice Kennedy hosted the Fifth Ohio Veterans Summit in 2019. Legal professionals, Veteran Service organizations and others came together to learn and collaborate; panel discussions were hosted, such as Veteran Service Commissions, non-profits, Veteran Treatment Courts and more. Major General John C. Harris, The Ohio National Guard Adjutant General, thanked attendees for their support and described challenges of this operational force.

Justice Kennedy's leadership, advocacy, and passion is changing the way the legal profession views and advocates for Servicemembers.

Veteran Champions Change the World

Hopefully, you see a pattern emerging. It starts with a civilian caring about our Servicemembers, a willing heart, a circle of influence, and a desire to help. Veteran Champions become informed, bring people together, offer encouragement and support, and most importantly, motivate and equip themselves and others to act. They don't just know and understand; they act and follow through to make a difference.

What can you do today to better support Veterans and improve quality of life, workforce, or community? This is how you change the world.

7. The Healthcare Community

Before we talk about what health care professionals can do as Veteran Champions, let's talk about how you, as an everyday citizen, can be more supportive. If you understand the Veterans' struggles, you'll see opportunities to extend a hand.

Despite the many excellent services provided by the VA, many Veterans don't seek this healthcare. Most don't know how to enroll or apply for service-connected disabilities. Some don't trust or believe in the VA system. Yes, it's complicated. But, accessibility to care, patient care services, and VA claims processing is greatly improving.

The VA provides America's largest integrated, wellness-focused health care. Their cutting-edge approach, *Whole Health*, centers around "what matters to you, not what is the matter with you." It's new and it's great stuff!

Did you know everybody who goes through the military should be evaluated to know if they have a service-connected disability? You don't have to be a healthcare professional to encourage a Veteran to go through the claims process.

According to a 2017 VA report, twelve of the twenty Veterans who take their lives daily are not enrolled in VA healthcare. Right here, Veteran Champions could make a huge impact.

As fellow citizens, we should recognize the signs, and know what to do if someone is suicidal. For the Veterans Crisis Line, dial 1-800-273-8255 and Press 1, or send a text message to 838255 to connect with a VA responder. If you want to help but aren't sure how, every VA needs volunteers. Call and find out what the VA has to offer.

What else can you do?

"Hey, Jenny, how are you doing during your husband's deployment? How are you doing supporting your husband? Your children? Yourself? What can I do?" That's what everyday heroes do. Being aware, knowledgeable, willing, and authentic. An informal, "How are you doing today? You know, I care about you. If I can help at all…" Initiate that conversation. You can listen. You can care. Offer to help and follow through!

A Veteran Champion makes it a point to know their neighbors who serve(d), has some understanding about military culture. They know what to say if they notice a struggling Veteran.

"Hey, I see you're struggling. What's going on?"

To learn more about what to say to a struggling Veteran, refer to Chapter 10.

As a civilian, it may take more courage to open that door. But it's worth it. They need you. Everybody can do something. No action is too small.

Behavioral Health Providers Learn Cultural Sensitivity

The Uniformed Services University (USU) of the Health Sciences, recognized that most civilian behavioral health providers don't understand military culture. To address this gap, the USU Center for Deployment Psychology, the Military Family Research Institute at Purdue University, state National Guards, and others, combined their efforts and developed a three-tiered course. It's designed to teach behavioral health providers how to treat Veterans, Servicemembers and their families with reintegration and deployment difficulties.

Since the development of Star Behavioral Health Providers (SBHP) in 2011, more than 1,000 Ohioans have participated. SBHP also hosts a clinician and community resources registry. I teach Tier One "Military Culture & Terminology: Enhancing Clinical Outcomes" that is open to everyone. I invite you to participate!

Thousands of families deal with the aftermath of war. If you're a Veteran or military spouse, how wonderful would it be if a Veteran Champion offered you their ear?

What if your behavior health provider understood how military service is hard on your family? Or helped you understand that what you're experiencing is normal? And not only asked culturally sensitive questions but offered evidenced-based solutions?

Needs More than Lip Service

Past President of the Ohio State Medical Association (OSMA) and past Chair of the Ohio Delegation to the American Medical Association (AMA), Dr. Hickey became aware of Veteran health care needs through the Ohio National Guard community outreach program. His dad and uncles were WW II Veterans. He had no personal military experience prior to participating in the Secretary of Defense's Joint Civilian Orientation Course and the Ohio National Guard's military immersion experience.

"I credit the Ohio National Guard with informing me about the needs of our Servicemembers and Military Connected Persons." Dr. Hickey remembers. "Until then, I had no idea."

Geographic dispersion and other difficulties can make accessing government-run health facilities difficult, if not impossible for Veterans. Dr. Hickey realized the Ohio physician community could be better informed about these needs and encouraged them to participate in or become an in-network TRICARE provider. As an Ophthalmology physician, he isn't personally situated as such to be a primary provider but provides specialty care when needed.

"I felt it essential to advocate for advantageous policies on the macro level that help Veterans, and to encourage individual local physicians to participate in Veteran care."

He carried this information to state physicians, and nationally to the American Medical Association (AMA). The first step was informing Ohio State Medical Association members about Veterans' care needs and ways to assist. Dr. Hickey took several policy proposals to the AMA House of Delegates meetings in the 2010s to support Veterans' healthcare access and improve physician participation in TRICARE Networks, and generally raised the visibility of these issues nationally.

The Ohio Delegation took resolutions to the AMA asking the VA to improve funding, reduce delays and increase access for care. Dr. Hickey was gratified by AMA's support and the actions taken by Congress to improve access and funding.

Generous, service-oriented physicians take concrete steps to improve access once they understand the obstacles. Even though more physicians practice as employees of large health systems, they can advocate for Veterans within their health systems. Communication is key.

Having reached the "elder statesman" stage of his medical career, Dr. Hickey speaks to support Veteran care issues whenever he can at annual meetings of OSMA as a past president and AMA as a current delegate for eight years.

"I'm less active in leadership now, but still in practice and personally do what I can." Dr. Hickey currently advocates for Veterans within his hospital health system in Central Ohio.

"We have to talk to each other and share our stories. Most busy people go through their lives focused on their own goals and needs and often miss what's right in front of them.

"Right after you thank a Veteran, ask what you, a physician, can do to make their life better. Service to Veterans needs to be more than just lip service."

Freedom is Never Free

Dr. Jennifer Hauler is one Veteran Champion on the Ohio Osteopathic Association (OOA), Board of Trustees with tremendous respect for those who serve and protect the freedoms that she enjoys. Her father, father-in-law, two uncles and husband all proudly served in the United States Armed Forces.

In 2013, Dr. Hauler jumped at the opportunity to participate in the Ohio National Guard TRICARE Working Group to identify obstacles Veterans face in seeking health care. She recruited peers to participate on the committee. Through the OOA, Jennifer increased awareness for optimizing physician resources to meet healthcare needs for Veterans.

Dr. Hauler developed strategies encouraging Ohio physicians to accept more patients using TRICARE—the healthcare program for Servicemembers and MCPs. She participated in discussions with Bill Dobbertin, Health Net Federal Services Director, Provider Network Management about regulatory barriers.

She encouraged the OOA to use conferences and publications to broaden awareness about the medical and psychological conditions related to military service, highlighting the need to care for more TRICARE beneficiaries.

For many years, OOA recruited osteopathic physicians to attend the Ohio National Guard military immersion experience. Briefings explained unit missions, Servicemember medical needs, and unique circumstances caused by deployments. One of which requires military families to change medical providers when shifting from civilian to military health insurance plans. Not only did dozens of OOA members participate, several physicians enlisted in National Guard or Reserve units!

Dr. Hauler's alma mater, Ohio University Heritage College of Osteopathic Medicine, Athens, has been a leader in identifying and meeting the healthcare needs of Veterans, with the guidance of Todd Fredricks, D.O.

Dr. Fredricks, a U.S. Army Colonel and State Surgeon for the West Virginia National Guard, discovered a lack of knowledge and understanding among civilian doctors concerning the physical and emotional trauma of combat. Dr. Fredericks produced and directed *The Veterans' Project.* The ninety-minute documentary has been viewed at special theater screenings, aired on PBS, in medical school classrooms, and at physician continuing education conferences, stimulating discussions about best practices for Veteran care.

"Educating, engaging and encouraging physicians—healthcare systems and care teams—to do our part is vital," Dr. Hauler said. We must understand Servicemembers and MCPs needs and the unique requirements of their healthcare plans.

Dr. Hauler understands that freedom is never free. She arranges and participates in Veteran's Day events, honors the fallen on Memorial Day, and supports organizations offering services to Veterans. She proudly displays a flag lapel pin— just another way she chooses to display her patriotism. At home, she teaches her son to honor the flag, the national anthem, and acknowledge and thank Veterans.

A passionate Veteran Champion, Dr. Hauler is committed to ensuring that physicians, providers, and healthcare systems embrace TRICARE. She believes that despite a tremendous amount of misinformation, TRICARE's requirements for providing patient care and receiving timely payment for services has greatly improved.

Over a four-year period, thanks to Dr. Hauler and Dr. Hickey, other leaders of Ohio's major healthcare associations, the number of in-network TRICARE providers in Ohio increased by over 40%!

Ohio's Traumatic Brain Injury (TBI) Pioneer

Dr. Chrisanne Gordon attended the Ohio National Guard community Town Hall meeting in May of 2009. There she met Ohio National Guard's "citizen-mobilizer" Major General Gregory L. Wayt. In response to 9/11, this commander hosted quarterly meetings across the state, educating and involving citizens in support of troops and their families.

Dr. Gordon had just completed a year voluntarily screening Veterans for TBI at the Chalmers P. Wylie VA Ambulatory Care Clinic. She uncovered the horrific disconnect between military and civilian healthcare systems' diagnosis and treatment of TBI. She told General Wayt she wanted to do more. He asked for her business card and, without breaking stride, called Colonel John C. Harris.

"John, this is a doctor and she wants to help with TBI—do something with her." Colonel Harris contacted her the next day and stood by her on the path that she continues today.

Prior to accepting her role as a TBI pioneer and advocate for Veterans, her relationship with the military was far removed. Her grandfather served in WWI, her father in WWII. Neither spoke of their service, nor attended Veteran events. However, they instilled in her patriotism and civil service at an early age.

Now, Dr. Gordon shapes the body of knowledge surrounding TBI, particularly its treatment and effects on Servicemembers lives. As a physical medicine and rehabilitation doctor, she experienced her own TBI giving her valuable insight, knowledge, and sensitivities about this misunderstood and poorly diagnosed war injury.

About 25% of returning warriors from Iraq and Afghanistan have TBI. Typically hidden, TBI exhibits no obvious injuries (bleeding) or overt medical signs (paralysis) but significantly impedes employment, education, and quality of life. These wounds are most often recognized by someone close to them, or an informed healthcare provider adept in assessing the subtle signs and symptoms.

In 2010, Dr. Gordon filmed *Operation Resurrection*. In 2012, she founded the nonprofit Resurrecting Lives Foundation to coordinate and advocate for successful transitions to a post-military life for TBI Veterans. In 2013, thanks to the assistance of Congressman Steve Stivers (then a Colonel in the Ohio Army National Guard), Dr. Gordon premiered her documentary on Capitol Hill. The film raised awareness about TBI and the issues facing Veterans struggling with brain injuries. Within the next month, legislation was produced that included TBI as part of the conversation about wounds of war.

She is nationally recognized and often quoted as a TBI expert and authored the book, *Turn the Lights On! A Physician's Personal Darkness of Traumatic Brain Injury (TBI) to Hope, Healing and Recovery*. Through her partnership with Cardinal Health, they collaborate on the hiring of Servicemembers with TBI.

Over the last decade, much has been learned about the brain. "For instance, science taught us that PTSD is, in fact, a chemically imbalanced pathway in the brain, serving as a survival mechanism," Dr. Gordon said. "Every activity is generated by a chemical and a receptor, and when we fully understand these cellular functions, we will be better physicians and healers."

She encourages assisting Veterans in the following ways:

- Welcome Servicemembers to your neighborhood; offer the support any new neighbor would appreciate.
- Introduce Veterans to community leaders in schools, churches, and other community organizations to make them feel welcome and transition easier. Organizations and individuals benefit from Veterans sharing lessons learned in military service, such as: Courage, Honor, Integrity, Duty, Loyalty, Respect, Selflessness, and Commitment.
- Contact lawmakers and advocate for Veterans' easy access to health care, education, and employment.

"Nearly two decades after the war in Afghanistan began, we continue falling short in treating our brain-injured Veterans," Dr. Gordon says, "a fact that is proven by the many co-morbidities witnessed every day in our young Veteran population: homelessness, incarceration, substance abuse, unemployment, and the worst and final complication: suicide.

"Anyone who suffers from a brain injury loses their voice," Dr. Gordon said. "Resurrecting Lives Foundation provides that voice and I will continue to do so until I lose mine."

It's Not Enough to Honor Veterans

Deborah Grassman learned lessons about personal peace in a unique way. She cared for over 10,000 dying Veterans throughout a thirty-year career as an advance practice hospice nurse at the VA in Tampa, Florida.

When hospice nurses help dying people review their lives, usually regrets surface. While caring for dying combat Veterans, Deborah and her team noticed that they exhibited re-occurring groupings of symptoms they later named "Soul Injury."

"Soul Injury" is a wound to our real self beyond our façade. These wounds—caused by unmourned loss and hurt, unforgiven guilt and shame and diminished self-compassion—stifle our full potential. They separate a person from who they're meant to be. Symptoms include emptiness, loss of meaning, feeling worthless or defective, and being disconnected from inner beauty.

The team helped combat Veterans forgive themselves for things they thought they should or should not have done, mourn and grieve. When this occurred, they often noticed visible liberation. Veterans needed less pain medication and became less agitated.

All too often, these dying Veterans poignantly asked, "Why couldn't I have learned this years ago? Why did I have to be dying?"

This was the impetus for starting the nonprofit Opus Peace. Co-founder and bereavement counselor Pat McGuire, Vietnam Veteran and Bronze Star Recipient Nurse Marie Bainbridge, Army Veteran Nurse Sheila Lozier, Deborah Grassman and "Shoku" decided these lessons needed to be shared with the rest of the world.

"Once we stop fearing loss, hurt, guilt, and shame," Deborah says, "we can stop minimizing and numbing our pain and start the healing process."

Me and hundreds of highly trained Ambassadors across the world, in the hospice community, other healthcare provider disciplines, clergy, and Veterans share these lessons with organizations and communities. Ambassadors teach people how to face emotional pain, experience it, and begin healing their Soul Injuries.

The team travels the world making presentations and offering soul restoration workshops. In every sense of the word, Opus Peace has created and is expanding an international Soul Injury movement, helping people heal.

Isn't it ironic that those trained for war are teaching us that through grieving and forgiveness we can heal and live in peace?

Through powerful communication techniques and expressions of grief through ceremony, Deborah helped Veterans express their feelings and start healing. Veterans might experience the loss of comrades who died in battle, loss of physical and mental health, or loss of the pre-war self.

Based upon Native American traditions used to welcome warriors home, Deborah's carefully designed Fallen Comrades Ceremony provides a safe sanctuary where Veterans acknowledge, mourn, and redeem loss. This ceremony acknowledges hardships, provides information about how to face these challenges and integrates the experience symbolically. Community members are encouraged to participate, giving civilians an important opportunity to recognize, honor, and share the burdens of war and military service.

Deborah shares these characteristics that distinguish Veterans from civilians:

- Veterans often acquire wisdom from having reckoned with trauma, stoicism, and addictions.
- Alcohol abuse or other "flighting" type of behaviors may be used to avoid confronting locked-up feelings or numb war-related traumatic memories.
- Stoicism ingrained in Servicemembers may interfere with their peaceful death and varies by degrees, depending on length and type of service.
- A combat Veteran's death may be further complicated by traumatic memories or paralyzing guilt.

Deborah credits Veterans for teaching her a vital lesson. "Once I learned how to listen to them, I learned to bear witness to their burdens of pain, shame, and the guilt they often carried."

Only a handful of healthcare providers specialize in caring for both dying and traumatized patients. She is one of the few.

For more than a decade, Deborah and her VA hospice nurse team provided Veteran pinning ceremonies to acknowledge military service. Hospice communities across the nation followed their example, starting the "We Honor Veterans" program.

To help a hurting Veteran, as a healthcare provider, volunteer, or family member:

- Don't reinforce stoicism or keeping a "stiff upper lip."
- Don't try to take their pain away. Instead, help them connect with the part of themselves that carries their pain. Encourage them to grieve.
- Instead of chiding them for their anger, say: "Tell me how you're hurting right now." To be able to listen and bear witness, you'll have to cultivate the courage to re-home your own pain. In the process, you'll both discover the vitality of your souls.
- Friends and family must grieve the loss of the person they used to know. After dangerous-duty assignments, a Veteran is forever changed. If families fail to grieve, conflicts will continually arise, adding pressure and guilt to the Veteran.
- Be a safe sanctuary for their stories. Encourage them to talk about their experiences, including losses they've sustained. Then listen—really listen.
- Act. It is not enough to honor Veterans.

Deborah's first book, *Peace at Last,* helps Veterans, their healthcare providers, caregivers, and family members understand the full impact of war, violence, and military culture, and offers them tools to reckon with it.

In her second book, *The Hero Within,* Deborah focuses on the role of emotional pain as an inevitable part of life. She teaches a 3-step process (abiding, reckoning, and beholding) and other techniques used to heal abuse, bring peace to broken relationships, face death, or assist in any life situation, and become more empowered.

To restore your own personal peace and be a Veteran Champion who can listen and bear witness, Deborah suggests, "Stop denying; stop numbing. Re-connect with the part of self carrying your pain and shame. Don't waste your suffering. Learn from it. Use it as the passport to your deepest self and you'll discover the power of your soul."

8. Community Influencers

You don't need to be an elected official, chairman of a civic organization or highly respected pillar of the community to be a Veteran Champion. Civilians who cultivate relationships with Veteran neighbors enhance their own quality of life as they decrease Veteran isolation. Not only are these relationships gratifying for those involved, they lay the foundation for the Veteran's sense of belonging and civic participation.

Research shows that Veterans are civic assets and provide communities valuable social capital.

In 2015, the American Enterprise Institute reported the results of the first-ever sociological examination of the civic health of Veterans. The empirical data unmistakably revealed that Veterans strengthen communities by talking with, trusting and doing favors for neighbors, working to fix problems in their neighborhood, participating in Service or Civic organizations, volunteering, donating to charity, engaging in local governments, and voting. And they do so at higher rates than their non-Veteran counterparts.

Whether you're an individual citizen or a recognized community leader, you can on your own or within your sphere of influence improve the lives of Veterans. And by so doing, strengthen communities.

Local community support for Veterans is critical. Why? Because, we change the world one person at a time. I radically believe that "everything is local." When you feel disconnected, lonely, or need a helping hand, wouldn't you prefer to connect with someone face to face? I would.

Do you know who the Veterans are where you live?

Some of our Veteran Champion stories show small gestures of genuine caring that make a big impact. Even the smallest act of kindness can reverberate years later.

Veterans Make Loyal Friends

Julie Stover comes from a long line of Servicemembers. Her father served in the Navy as did her brother and several cousins. An additional half dozen relatives served in other branches. When she found herself in Jacksonville, Florida she and her husband were 800 miles from home but right in the heart of a Navy town.

Julie and her husband were newlyweds and at the holidays, rather than make the trek back to Ohio during the unpredictable winter weather, they invited others who were also far from home to share meals, starting with a dual military couple who lived next door.

"We didn't always have a lot of money, but we always had plenty of food. When we had meals together, I enjoyed hearing their stories."

The circle expanded to include Tim, an active duty sailor, and through her retail job, Julie met Karyl, a co-worker and Navy wife whose father had been an Army chaplain.

"We became close. Karyl always called me her lucky star," Julie said. "I didn't know what she meant, but it made me smile. We hung out a lot for several years."

Eventually, Julie's military friends got new orders and they all moved to other locations. But, thanks to social media, she's remained friends with the sailor wife, and Karyl to this day—over thirty years later.

Ever since those days, Julie has made it a personal mission to keep an eye out for military people and thank them for their service, buy them a cup of coffee, and even lunch.

"I owe them so much: especially for my freedom. Years later, after my divorce, Karyl sent me a plane ticket to visit her in New Mexico. It was one of the highlights of my life. Over the years, I've found military people to be loyal, honest, and giving friends. I still have a lot of military people in my circle and I wouldn't want it any other way."

Julie connected over meals, initially to brighten holidays of Servicemembers who might otherwise be alone. In return, they enjoyed deep lasting friendships, were "there" for each other and watched each other's kids grow up. Veterans added meaning to her life, and she added to theirs. Another win-win!

Chamber Leader Values Veteran Talent

Janet Tressler-Davis is President and CEO of the Westerville Area Chamber of Commerce. Through her transformative leadership of over twenty-seven years, Janet built the Chamber into one of the region's most valuable resources for small businesses as well as one of the nation's leading professional organizations. As a forward-thinking leader, she fosters understandings about military culture and builds bridges for Veterans with employers.

Janet, a speaker, and widely respected, award-winning community leader appreciates what Veterans bring to the workforce. Over the last decade, she's embraced opportunities to broaden awareness about the value of their talent among chamber executives, community partners, and small business owners.

As a part of Westerville WorkWISE, a new community-wide workforce alliance, Janet invited me and the Central Ohio Workforce Consultant from the Ohio Department of Veterans Services to inform community leaders about Veteran employment and employer hiring and retention resources. Including these resources in their "asset mapping'" of workforce providers is an important first step. Identifying resources for hiring and leveraging Veteran skillsets will help local businesses narrow workforce skills gaps.

Janet was instrumental in helping design Central Ohio's Veterans Employment and Talent Solutions, a regional public/private workforce partnership under development. Its goal is to promote awareness about the value of Veteran talent and streamline the delivery of Veteran hiring and retention resources and solutions.

And now, the Westerville Area Chamber is creating a "Veteran Champion Award" to recognize businesses that best support Veterans.

In the past, Janet invited the Ohio National Guard Community Outreach office to connect with employers and regional executives at a multi-chamber business expo. She invited us to talk about the value of Veteran talent and invite business leaders to learn more. The outreach office hosted an Employer Advisory Council forum focused on small-and medium-sized business and invited chamber members to military immersion experiences. I credit all these activities to Janet's influential and visionary leadership.

Currently, one Coast Guard Veteran works for the Chamber.

"I didn't hire him specifically because he was a Veteran," Janet said. "I hired him because he's disciplined and honest."

Janet encourages chamber leaders to do these things to help businesses be more creative finding and recruiting qualified talent:

- Invite experts to educate members about sourcing Veterans, emphasizing how military service hones skills needed in the civilian workforce, and how to translate military occupations to the private sector.
- Share what you learn about Veteran talent (and the associated resources) among your networks to get the word out.

Another big win: Veteran Champion elected officials are exploring how to officially designate Westerville as Veteran-Friendly.

Mayor Gives Veterans a Strong Voice

Michael B. Coleman served as the 52nd mayor of Columbus and achieved the distinction of being the longest-serving mayor in Columbus' history—fifteen years. His son, John David, served as a sergeant in the United States Marine Corps and in the Army as a Green Beret.

"There are approximately 130,000 Veterans in our region, and we deal regularly with the issues they and their families face," said Mayor Coleman. "I believe that it's important that Veterans have a strong voice in my administration, working every day to coordinate our City's services and make sure that we're doing the right thing, not only for employees with military backgrounds but also for all the residents of Columbus who serve the nation through the United States Armed Forces."

In 2005, Coleman appointed the first full-time Veteran Affairs Coordinators in a City Municipality, Mr. Richard "Rick" A. Isbell, who served seven years in the U.S. Air Force. Prior to working for the city, he worked five years as a Disabled Veterans Outreach Specialist for the Ohio Department of Jobs and Family Services. He designed and implemented the Veterans First Campaign for Ohio.

For over eleven years, Rick served as a liaison to Columbus' Veteran community, coordinated the activities of the Mayor's Veterans Advisory Council and local Veteran's events, advocated for Veterans benefits and issues, and guided internal policy for returning Servicemembers who were city employees.

I was honored to work alongside Rick for many years. He's a consummate professional with a powerful ability to build trusting relationships. As a world-class servant leader, he referred countless Veterans to needed community support resources. His approach also fostered engagement and cooperation among the Central Ohio Veteran community. Outcomes realized by Mayor Coleman and Rick include:

- Winning the 2013 Secretary of Defense Employer Support Freedom Award
- Participation on the Veteran Board that conceived of and created the National Veterans Memorial and Museum

- City programmers across the nation adopting many of Columbus' Veterans Affairs best practices
- A managers and supervisors manual showing how to support Guard and Reserve employees before, during, and after deployment
- Nearly twelve percent of Columbus' workforce are (or were) military members
- Hosting ten public patriotic and Veteran events per year

Mayor Coleman's and Rick's strong partnership spurred the creation of municipal Veterans Affairs programs nationally and improved Central Ohio's quality of life, workforce, and community.

A Policy Wonk Does More

Before becoming president and owner of Comprehensive Policy Research Solutions, LLC, Erik F. Yassenoff worked on developing and implementing public policy for twenty years at the federal, state, and local levels. Erik's experience includes five years working on Capitol Hill, serving on two Ohio Governors' policy staffs, and managing the General Services Division at the Ohio Department of Administrative Services.

As Erik concluded his eight-year term on Upper Arlington City Council and started his Republican Candidacy for the Ohio House, he volunteered to lead the redesign of the Upper Arlington Veterans Memorial.

He was the liaison, doing the lion's share of planning, fundraising and coordination. Simply put, the revival of the community memorial was possible because of his leadership. This memorial honors local Veterans and gives all residents a sense of pride and patriotism.

While a candidate for the Ohio House, I persuaded Erik to include Veteran issues in his campaign platform. When the race concluded, (and years after), Erik and I drafted legislation to leverage Veteran talent as a primary solution for Ohio's workforce skills gap. Attracting and retaining Veteran talent is as an economic development imperative! We'd like to see more robust strategies to draw and keep Veteran talent in Ohio, and employer education to help them become "Veteran- Ready."

We've met with state legislators, staffers, and agency directors to clarify best practices and cultivate support. Workforce legislation alongside other proposed quality of life measures would bring and keep Servicemembers in Ohio and give the state a national advantage.

Erik undertook this project and continues this quest as a volunteer and patriotic citizen, not as a state legislator. He wants to do more to honor those who serve.

For Veteran Champions wanting to shape state legislation, Erik suggests following these tips:

- Draft a legislative proposal using the code of your state. Legislators are more receptive when you provide legislative language even if it goes through many changes.
- Know what your state already does and what other states do. Members of any state's general assembly are always interested in seeing how they compare to other states and often like to emulate other states' best practices.
- You need data to prove your point and demonstrate that there is a need.
- Plan for the long haul. Understand that the legislative process takes time.

"My driving force to support Veterans comes from my connection with family members who served in the Armed Forces, the events of 9/11, and my regret for not having served in the military while others my age did."

9. The Education Community

While Military life is the choice of parents, it isn't the choice of their children. Though the military experience can positively translate to more adaptable children and eventually flexible adults, a downside is often feeling isolated and "different from other kids." Supporting the children of active duty, Guard and Reserve personnel is another arena where Veteran Champions are needed—and appreciated by their parents.

Nearly two million military-connected kids have parents serving on active duty. They have a unique view of American public education because they move every one to three years. This could be from state to state or overseas to foreign countries. A military child's life is one of transitions: deployments, separations, and adjustments.

The DOD reports that the average K-12 military-connected child will attend six to nine schools. As reported by the Military Child Education Coalition (MCEC), of the 800,000+ children scattered throughout the USA, seventy-five percent are below age thirteen, over half are under five. These students face issues such as gaps and overlaps in curriculum, course placement disruption, different graduation requirements plus the emotional and social challenges of relocation. This includes leaving friends and supportive social activities to start over. Addressing these hurdles has become a top priority for military families across the nation, some schools and state public education systems.

The U.S. Air Force recently incentivized states to resolve these hurdles. In early 2020, they announced that future basing decisions will include evaluating public education systems, academic performance, school climate, and programs that ease transitions of military kids.

MCEC, a national non-profit, works to optimize school conditions for kids of active duty Servicemembers. To help them thrive in the face of transition and separation. They offer resources and programming for parents and children, trainings for teachers and school administrators and this spectrum of things to consider when supporting military children:

- They're just kids!
- Transitioning from military to civilian life is tough for military kids too.
- The first two weeks in a new school is especially tough—give special attention.
- They may be in a caregiving family with a parent who is wounded, ill, or injured.

- Moving can be the best or worst thing — caring adults matter.
- Separation from a parent is never easy.
- Moving and changing schools means academic challenges.
- For those with special needs, transitions can be more complicated.
- They're proud of their parents' military service.
- Over forty percent will enlist someday!

Children of Guard and Reserve members face different challenges. They're surrounded by civilian support systems, until a parent is deployed. When this occurs, they often feel alone and misunderstood. More than 34,000 military youth from all branches of the armed forces reside in Ohio.

Military Family Readiness programs help military-connected families prepare for, withstand, and adapt after deployments. Learning that your family is "suddenly military" and enduring through the deployment cycle is challenging. Fortunately, many children also receive support from the Ohio State University Extension 4-H Youth Development program, Ohio Military Kids.

The innovative program Purple Star Schools addresses needs of all military kids. It began in

Ohio as the brainchild of Navy Veteran Pete LuPiba, Ohio's Commissioner for the Military Children Interstate Compact Commission. Starting with a handful of schools in 2017, more than 190 Ohio schools carry the Purple Star Schools designation, showing they're military friendly in the following ways:

- Having a staff point of contact for military students and families
- School liaisons completing professional development on special considerations for military students and their families
- Maintaining a dedicated page on the school website with military family resources
- Conducting one of these activities: the school board passing a resolution in support of military children, and/or hosting a military appreciation event
- Identifying military students (this isn't easy)
- Informing staff members who military students are and their special considerations

Middle School Teacher Cares about Military Kids

A few years ago, Michelle Lewis visited her son at his Air Force base. They stopped at the USO in San Francisco, California. He appreciated what they did for active duty military and suggested that she volunteer for them after finishing her dissertation. Not only did she volunteer for the USO of Central and Southern Ohio at their airport lounges, she supported Columbus Honor Flight and military appreciation events in the public-school district where she teaches.

Michelle's colleague, Army Reservist 2Lt. Jason Durell emailed school district employees asking if anyone was interested in starting a committee focused on supporting military-connected students and their families. Michelle responded, which led to the creation of Olentangy Military Families Committee (OMFC). In this forum, interested civilians, Servicemembers and community members brainstorm for ways to help military connected families in the area. "It was eye-opening," she said, "to discover so many Servicemembers on staff and in the community."

Michelle soon became involved with the Purple Star Schools program. She served on their

Advisory Board and later became editor of the quarterly Purple Star Bulletin, which informs the liaisons in Purple Star Schools.

She got involved with the Military Interstate Children's Compact Commission, an agreement among all fifty states that gives these students rights as they move, or PCS (Permanent Change of Station). This eases student's transition and alleviates some parental stress.

At Hyatts Middle School, Michelle meets monthly with fourteen of twenty military kids for breakfast. One had this to say about the group, "I look forward to the meetings because I feel like everyone has almost the same experiences as me. I feel like they understand me."

One summer, she and the military kids painted the Hyatts Military Wall of Honor. As a daily visual reminder of how connected the school community is to the Armed Forces, staff and students place memorial bricks on the wall in October and November.

On their first field trip, the kids were accompanied by "their" Veteran, Mr. Richard Doritty to the National Veterans Memorial and Museum. He secured funding from Veteran organizations to cover entry costs and lunch for these students.

"I loved the museum," one said, "and seeing how the military affected things. It impacted me seeing what people like my dad did while he wasn't home."

Michelle accepted the role of Military Outreach for Living History Day at her school. Twenty years ago, Nancy Braun Poliseno created Living History Day to connect the military community with their students. As a day with no regular classes, a ceremony is held to honor more than one-hundred military guests, and grant students an opportunity to listen to their stories.

As an Air Force mom, Michelle is familiar with the sacrifices of those who serve. She's honored to serve the military by helping teachers learn about MCP and solve problems that better the lives of their children.

Some best ways to support military kids are:

- Know who they are and care about them.
- Understand military culture and learn to speak their language.
- Participate in military sponsored educator's tours and workshops. These provide opportunities to spend time on a military base and to interact with personnel at all levels, from recruit to general.

Veterans in Higher Education

The opportunity to pursue higher education after service is important to many Servicemembers. They often leave high school to serve our country while their counterparts go off to college. Unprecedented opportunities exist for Veteran Champions to create welcoming environments and promote the success of Servicemembers pursuing degrees. From fast-track college programs to scholarships, including educational and community building events.

The Ohio Department of Higher Education laid the educational cornerstone for Ohio's commitment to Veterans. Key pieces of legislation include:

• In 2009, "Ohio GI Promise," House Bill 480, was passed to "make Ohio the most Veteran-Friendly state in the country for higher education." This allows Veterans to skip the twelve-month residency requirement at Ohio's public colleges and universities.

• In 2013, Governor John R. Kasich signed Executive Order 2013-05K to support Ohio's Veterans by ensuring they receive the appropriate credit and credentialing for their military training and experience—and streamline occupational licensing processes for Veterans while ensuring military education, skills training, and experience are taken into account.

• In 2014, House Bill 488 required Ohio's higher education institutions to expand academic transition support for Veterans through these kinds of services:

- o A single point of contact on campus
- o Priority registration
- o Support policies that survey Servicemembers and Veterans to identify their specific needs
- o Student-led groups
- o Integration of existing career services to help Veteran students find civilian work

Becoming Who They're Meant to Be

Assistant Dean, Strategic Initiatives and Community Engagement, Lisa Durham—a military spouse—has championed Veterans and their families for over a decade.

"When my husband deployed to Iraq, I saw firsthand our own struggles as well as that of those in his unit. Upon his return, the readjustment period was difficult. At times it still is. He came back different. And I changed while he was gone."

Through her work at the Ohio State University College of Social Work, alumni working with Veterans and Military Connected Persons were invited to revamp the Social Work major curriculum; to better serve those desiring to work with the military community.

Lisa established a certificate program and is creating a formal track within the Master of Social Work (MSW) program, to better inform professionals working with Veterans. Lisa's work with college development teams secured a full scholarship ($10,000/year) for a Veteran student and increased field placement opportunities for MSW students with the VA and Ohio National Guard.

"When I retire, I'll look back on this work and my relationships with Servicemembers as the most meaningful of my life. I'm helping Veterans become who they're meant to be so they can do work that is most meaningful to them."

Lisa served as board member of the nonprofit, Run Down the Demons. Started by one of their students, now an alumnus, their mission is to expand awareness about PTSD and promote suicide prevention. She hosted a state conference on Servicemember suicide, inviting national speakers in social work, mental health, and other healthcare disciplines.

With the OSU Military and Veterans Services Office, Lisa co-hosted a campus screening of the movie *Thank You for Your Service*. This included a discussion with its author David Finkel. They also co-sponsored an educational campus event with Run Down the Demons, General Mark Graham, and his wife Carol. The Grahams lost two military sons: one to an IED, another to suicide.

"I see and feel their pain, their strength and commitment, and most importantly their desire to help other Veterans. I don't know how to put into words how much I respect every Soldier."

Lisa offers these important guidelines for supporting Veterans:

- Never ever ask if they killed someone!
- A Veteran will tell their story when they're ready. As trust grows, they'll let you in to the level they are comfortable. Respect that.
- Never assume you know, understand, or "have a clue" what a Veteran or family member is going through. Each person is unique. Every experience is unique. Honor that.

"I've met the most amazing people through this work," she says," I'm so honored to be a Veteran Champion. I hope others join me. There's so much work to do."

Veteran Champions go Beyond, "Thank You for Your Service."

I know how much our country loves those who serve(d) in the Armed Forces. By reading these Veteran Champion stories it is my hope that you've been inspired and have already begun considering ways that you might partner with and serve Veterans and Military Connected Persons. As I've stated throughout the book, the relationships forged are life affirming and life changing. Your kindness and concern for our military is greatly appreciated and never wasted.

You've learned many heartfelt and effective ways Veteran Champions make a difference. My hope is that through your actions you'll share your gratitude with even more Veterans and go beyond "Thank you for your service."

Being a Veteran Champion isn't rocket science, it's people science.

10. Resources

Department of Veterans Affairs
Emergency Resources

• **Veteran's Crisis Line: www.veteranscrisisline.net**
(800) 273-8255 (press 1) text 838255 24 hours a day/
7 days a week

• **Military Sexual Trauma (MST) Support:**
VA offers free counseling services for Military Sexual
Trauma survivors. You don't have to be enrolled in VA
Health Care to access MST services. Call your local Medi-
cal Center or Vet Center. At Medical Centers, ask for the
MST coordinator. https://www.va.gov/find-locations/

• **Women Veterans Call Center**
www.womenshealth.va.gov
(855) VA WOMEN (855) 829-6636
M-F, 8 AM–10 PM EST Sat, 8 AM–6:30 PM EST

• **National Call Center for Homeless Vets**
www.veteranscrisisline.net
(877) 424-3838 24 hours a day/ 7 days a week

• **VA Caregiver Support Line www.caregiver.va.gov**
(855) 260-3274 8 AM–8 PM EST

- **Find help near you:**

Locate your nearest VA Medical Facility, Regional Benefits Office, Regional Loan Center, Vet Center, National Cemetery, and other VA facilities at
https://www.va.gov/find-locations/

National Suicide Prevention Line:
https://suicidepreventionlifeline.org/help-yourself/veterans/

Stories From Veterans Who Sought help:
www.maketheconnection.net

WHAT TO SAY TO A STRUGGLING VETERAN
To validate emotional pain:

- "You've been struggling a lot lately."

- "You've had a hard go of it."

- "It takes a lot to go through what you've been through."

- "You've endured a lot."

- "I guess you're pretty weary with all that's happened."

- "Tell me about the difficulties you've been having."

- "Of all these difficulties, what is the hardest for you to deal with?"

To allow a safe place for tears:

- "It's okay to cry."
- "Your tears are safe here."
- "Don't choke down your tears. When you feel the lump in your throat, release it through tears."

Things NOT to say. Platitudes minimize feelings.

- "Count your blessings."
- "You've got to look on the bright side."
- "God never gives you more than you can handle."
- "Something good will come out of this."
- "You were just following orders."
- "How could you do that to yourself?"
- "What is wrong with you?"

IF A VETERAN HAS THOUGHTS OF SUICIDE:
Demonstrations of these behaviors requires immediate attention:

- Searching for ways to kill him or herself
- Talking about death, dying or suicide. You may hear:
  - "I can't go on like this."
  - "No one can help me."

- "My family would be better off if I wasn't here."
- Self-destructive behavior such as:
  - Increasing drug/alcohol abuse, unsafe use of weapons, etc.
  - Exhibits extreme emotional outbursts (loud crying, yelling)

DO NOT leave this struggling Veteran alone!

If you don't see the behaviors above, ask:
- "Are you thinking about killing yourself?" Start a conversation to help him/her open up.
- "When did you first start feeling like this?"
- "Did something happen that made you begin feeling this way?"

Simple and encouraging feedback goes a long way to show support and encourage help-seeking.
- "You're not alone, even if you feel like you are. I'm here for you, and I want to help you in any way I can."
- "It may not seem possible right now, but the way you're feeling will change."
- "I might not be able to understand exactly what you're going through or how you feel, but I care about you and want to help."

Veteran Crisis Line at 1-800-273-8255, Press 1, Text 838255 or VeteransCrisisLine.net/Chat

Call if the Veteran has any of these warning signs:
- Hopelessness, feeling like there is no way out
- Anxiety, agitation, sleeplessness, mood swings
- Feeling like there is no reason to live
- Rage or anger
- Engaging in risky activities without thinking
- Increasing alcohol or drug abuse
- Withdrawing from family and friends

***

Other websites and links:

* Vanguard Veteran
VanguardVeteran.com kathy@vanguardveteran.com
Facebook https://www.facebook.com/VanguardVet/
YouTube https://www.youtube.com/channel/UC2fg-2idCgf-QUoZ4zZ9Y6Q
LinkedIn
https://www.linkedin.com/company/25029573/admin/
or https://www.linkedin.com/in/lt-col-ret-kathy-lowrey-gallowitz-0618314/

* Veteran Interfaith Bridge
https://www.veteraninterfaithbridge.org

* Military Child Education Coalition
https://www.militarychild.org

* Opus Peace https://opuspeace.org

* PsychArmor Veteran community educational resource
https://psycharmor.org